To my good friend Mac
and to the great times we've had in Scottsdale, Arizona

Contents

CONTENTS

Foreword

by Andy Dorf

Baseball was the last professional sport to come to the valley of the sun.

Spring training has always attracted both visitors and residents. Fans have a great opportunity to get up close and meet the players during this time. With so much interest generated by the boys of summer, one wonders why it took so long for baseball to come full-time to Phoenix. Perhaps one reason it took so long was spring training itself. People came to see their teams play. With the influx of new residents from all over the country, their loyalties remained with their home teams. Another factor that comes to mind is that Phoenix already had three professional sports teams. The Phoenix Suns—who have been, year in and year out, a perennial powerhouse—are regularly playoff contenders and very well attended. We have also had the Arizona Cardinals who, on the other hand, have not achieved much success and have not been well attended. The other professional sports team, oddly enough, was the Phoenix Coyotes hockey team. The big question had to be: would the market become too saturated with a fourth professional team? While the fantastic growth of Phoenix meant there was potentially a large audience, the question for owners and management would be: how would fans allocate their sports entertainment dollars?

When baseball came to the desert full-time, it was a dream come true.

Time has passed, and we can now appreciate how sweet it can be on top of the sports world. It has been several years since that unforgettable season of 2001.

How could anyone expect the Diamondbacks to be both a winner and a contender for a World Series championship so early in their existence? What transpired between 1998, the year they arrived in Phoenix, and 2001, when they cashed in and won a World Series title? With the magic of free agency and frequent movement of players, this dream became a reality. Putting a winner together quickly was made possible by acquiring big-name players who could deliver. Players like Randy "the Big Unit" Johnson, one of the more dominant left-handers in the game, and Curt Schilling, a right-hander, provided one of, if not the best, one-two pitcher combinations the game has ever seen. Many others contributed to this magical season and the team's early successes. Some of those players included Mark Grace, Matt Williams, Erubiel Durazo, David Dellucci, Jay Bell, and Junior Spivey. I would be remiss if I did not mention a guy like Craig Counsell, who could play anywhere in the infield and is a true team player, and the ultimate fan favorite, Luis Gonzalez, who in my mind is the original Diamondback and the face of this franchise. Although the face will now have to change because Luis is no longer playing with the team. There were many other ballplayers who played a major role in the early success and development of this franchise. To all those I did not mention, I apologize.

This championship team came together because of Jerry Colangelo's belief that Phoenix was a major league city and therefore should have major league baseball. For Colangelo, just having a team was not enough, he wanted a winner.

To accomplish his dream, he needed a courageous manager, someone with grit, guts, and heart. This was Bob Brenly, a player's manager, someone who demanded respect and hard work. As a fan, I thank you for sticking with your game plan, regardless of what others thought. Your instincts, intuition, and feeling for the game have been missed. Thanks also to Jerry Colangelo and management for raising and spending the funds necessary to bring a winning product to Phoenix.

This payroll gave the Diamondbacks instant credibility. Success was achieved because of management, talent, fan support, hard work, and luck.

The Arizona Diamondbacks did the unthinkable in a post-9/11 World Series. The New York Yankees were heavily favored, not only sentimentally but realistically as well. They had talent, experience, tradition, and the biggest payroll in baseball. On the other hand, the Diamondbacks had nothing to lose and everything to gain. This particular D'backs team stepped up to the challenge. In doing this, they set a new standard of excellence. Current and future teams will have high expectations. Who knows what the future will hold? One can only hope for more World Series championships.

The season of 2001 proved that dreams do come true. Now the players, management, and fans hope for more successes. It is important, however, to realize that sports and life are very similar. They both have highs and lows. I guess life and sports really are an emotional roller coaster. It's how you deal with the ups and downs that defines you as a person. In sports, as well, how you deal with success and failure defines a team. Having covered Diamondbacks successes, I am hopeful for the future. So I say with all my heart, as a fan first and a media guy second, good luck now and in the future to the Arizona Diamondbacks. I won't forget how sweet it once was and how sweet it can be.

Andy Dorf is a respected sports radio talk show host with a national show based out of Phoenix, Arizona. He is also a TV personality.

Acknowledgments

Thanks to Tom Bast, Jess Paumier, Amy Reagan, Linc Wonham, Morgan Hrejsa, Phil Springstead, Scott Rowan, Bill Swanson, Kris Anstrats, Mike Emmerich, Mitch Rogatz, and all the great folks at Triumph Books and Random House Publishing for having faith in me. Thanks also to my agent, Craig Wiley. I want to thank the Diamondbacks, a classy organization all the way. Thank you to Mike McNally, Greg Salvatore, Barry Gossage, Miguel Batista, Dave Lumia, Pedro Gomez, and Dan Bickley.

Thanks to Karen Peterson for website support. Thanks to John Horne and Pat Kelly at the Baseball Hall of Fame.

Of course, my thanks as always go out to my daughter, Elizabeth Travers; my parents, Don and Inge Travers; and to my Lord and savior, Jesus Christ, who has shed his grace on thee, and to whom all glory is due!

Arizona:
A Baseball Tradition

The state of Arizona was, for all practical purposes, the Wild West well into the 20th century. After World War II, with population growth shifting to the Sun Belt, the state grew dramatically.

Many servicemen trained in the state (including a major Officers Candidate School at the University of Arizona), settling there after the war. Las Vegas, located a few hours away, became a tourist destination. Jet travel had an enormous effect. President Dwight D. Eisenhower signed a highway bill that created modern roads, connecting cities with each other.

Sports popularity grew around the Arizona State Sun Devils, the Arizona Wildcats, and spring training baseball. Construction magnate Del Webb built spring training complexes (as well as major league parks in other cities, chief among them Anaheim Stadium). Webb brought in the New York Yankees. Horace Stoneham's Giants trained at Casa Grande, where a resort was built around the baseball facilities.

In 1951 the Yankees and Giants switched spring training sites. Legend has it that young Yankees *shortstop* Mickey Mantle threatened the health of many a fan sitting along the first-base line with his wild throws.

By the 1960s, there was a large contingent of big-league clubs training in Arizona (the Angels were in nearby Palm Springs, California). They called it the Cactus League, as opposed to the larger Grapefruit League in Florida. Since that time, a number of teams have made the switch from Florida to Arizona for several reasons.

Florida rains a lot and is more humid. Many years ago, Florida had a Jim Crow element to it that Arizona never had, although that problem is long gone. But the Grapefruit League was always spread

Before the Diamondbacks, Arizona baseball fans had to get their fix at college games or spring training games. In this photo, Willie Mays of the New York Giants makes a spectacular catch in a spring workout at the Giants' Phoenix training base in 1956.

throughout the state, making for long bus trips. With some exceptions, the Cactus League is centered in and around metropolitan Phoenix. It is a convenient league for the clubs and, especially, the fans. They can get a hotel room in town and, within a week, make the rounds of all the teams training in the area. And night beckons the "Neon League," as my good pal and ex-A's teammate Dennis Gonsalvez calls it.

"We were stars in the Neon League," Dennis says.

The success and popularity of college sports—and college baseball—offers as much of an explanation for sports growth as anything. ASU and U of A developed into major college programs. Legendary Sun Devils football coach Frank Kush built Arizona State into a powerhouse in the late 1960s and early 1970s. The Western Athletic Conference became a force to be reckoned with, mirroring the wide-open passing offenses of the fledgling American Football League.

Collegiate baseball was small-time, with the exception of the University of Southern California, until the 1960s. Texas, Oklahoma, California, Minnesota, and Ohio State fielded excellent teams, but the college game was played on glorified high school fields in front of friends, family, and hard-core fans sitting on wooden benches.

Bobby Winkles had a vision for Arizona State, starting the baseball program from scratch in 1959. Winkles knew that the warm weather meant he could practice all fall and winter, then begin a full slate of games in February. He foresaw fans escaping the cold to enjoy baseball and sunshine. He knew the growth of Phoenix meant more high schools would be built, thus providing an ever-greater talent pool. The attraction of college baseball, which was in full swing well before the big leaguers started playing exhibition games, was a major allure for "snow birds" who chose to make Arizona their new home.

Winkles, USC coach Rod Dedeaux, and a few others started sending their players to Alaska to play in a competitive summer league. By the time a young man had played three or four years in a good college program, he had gained valuable experience, been well scouted, and received an education. It was a better route than the minors.

Within six short years, Winkles transformed Sun Devils baseball from a glorified club sport into a national power. His 1965 College

TRIVIA

Answers to the trivia questions are on pages 159–160.

World Series champions are still considered one of the great teams ever. Superstars like Rick Monday, Sal Bando, and Reggie Jackson were drafted out of Tempe. When they went onto big league success, everybody knew precisely where they had come from.

Packard Stadium was built. It became a showcase for college baseball; a fabulous, lighted facility with all the amenities of a miniaturized big-league stadium. Large, enthusiastic crowds flocked to Sun Devils games.

A couple hours down the road, former big-league infielder Jerry Kindall built a program to rival Winkles at the University of Arizona. In the 1970s Winkles rode his college success to managerial positions with the California Angels and Oakland A's. Kindall and new Arizona State coach Jim Brock had dynasties in Tempe and Tucson. Eventually, the great Barry Bonds was attracted by the ASU juggernaut. He became an All-American under Brock.

College baseball popularity grew in direct proportion to Arizona State and Arizona. The College World Series became a regularly televised event. Other programs—Miami, Texas, Texas A&M, Oklahoma State, just to name a few—built baseball palaces to rival and exceed the facilities at ASU, USC, and the early powerhouses.

Another phenomenon occurred, and its effect cannot be ignored. Phoenix, Arizona, was transformed from a geriatric community of retirement homes, resorts, and golf courses into a thriving college town, then a Mecca of youth and beauty. Year after year, thousands of kids migrated from the freezing climes of Kansas, Iowa, and thereabouts to enjoy an academic atmosphere in the desert warmth.

Naturally, many beautiful, tanned young girls populated the ASU campus. Bars sprouted up all around Tempe, built on the foundation of their presence. Then those kids grew up and found jobs. "Grown-up" bars sprouted up in nearby Scottsdale, an upscale suburb long known for its golf courses and wealth. Over time, Scottsdale became a nightlife capital to rival Miami's South Beach. Word spread. As if drawn by magic waters, to quote James Earl Jones in *Field of Dreams*, people came in search of Nirvana in the form of sexy women, happening clubs, and eternal youth.

Built side by side with this hedonistic world was a mostly Republican, business-friendly, growth-oriented political class. They were conservative in the Barry Goldwater tradition, churchgoers who wanted to build a clean city, but not so prudish as to dissuade the nightlife crowd from having a little fun. They saw the future in these wide-open desert spaces and, like Las Vegas, set forth to build and build and build. Out here they could do that in a way the old, closed-in Eastern cities—hemmed in by rivers, harbors, and other natural barriers—could not.

A can-do attitude came to prevail in Arizona. Political power came to the state, first in the form of Senator Goldwater, who symbolized the conservative movement; later in the person of Senator John McCain, a more moderate Republican whose aspirations are the White House Goldwater failed to attain.

The kind of people who populate Arizona tend to be those who buy into the American Dream. They see unlimited potential and are not hampered by old boundaries of class or race. It was this mindset that built the state. Over time, big-league sports came to them: the NBA Suns, the NFL Cardinals, the NHL Coyotes, the Fiesta Bowl...and finally the biggest prize of them all, the Diamondbacks.

DID YOU KNOW . . . That spring training originally developed out of barnstorming and vacations? New York Giants manager John McGraw liked to travel to sunny California in the off-seasons, where baseball is played year-round. He discovered catcher Chief Meyer, a Native American from the desert east of Los Angeles. Walter Johnson was first seen pitching for an oil rigging team in Fullerton. McGraw started taking his teams to the warm South for preseason training; Hot Springs, Arkansas; Florida; Georgia; and other locales. Babe Ruth and Lou Gehrig also barnstormed to Western states in the winter, as did the Negro League players.

Birth Pangs in the Desert

On December 7, 1941, the owner of the St. Louis Browns was pre-pared to announce his plans to move to Los Angeles, California. On that day, the Japanese bombed Pearl Harbor. California, it was feared, was their next target. The plans were nixed.

In October of 1947 fighter ace Chuck Yeager broke the sound barrier in the skies above Southern California. Jet travel was now fully operational. A few years later, President Eisenhower signed a comprehensive highway bill. America was now a mobile nation. The West would never be the same.

In 1958 the Dodgers and Giants moved to California. Three years later, expansion came: Los Angeles got a second team. By 1962 big-league baseball was now in Houston and Minnesota. New York and Washington replaced franchises that had left.

Expansion continued. In 1969: Seattle, Kansas City, San Diego, and Montreal. 1977: Seattle (replacing the Pilots-turned-Brewers) and Toronto. 1993: Colorado and Florida. 1998: Arizona and Tampa Bay.

Expansion was always about money: bigger TV markets, more merchandising, a larger slice of the pie. There are many purists who have argued that expansion dilutes the talent pool, but there is little real evidence to support this theory. The talent pool has grown tremendously. Population growth has occurred, but more than any-thing, a huge influx of foreign talent has come to baseball from Latin America. To a lesser extent, players come from Asia, Canada, and Australia.

While many lament that kids "don't play baseball anymore," the fact is that in the "good ol' days" boys lived on farms or inner cities with no organized little leagues or high school teams. The mythology

After days of delays, a 1,200-ton steel truss is raised from the ground in downtown Phoenix to become part of the backbone of the Arizona Diamondbacks' new ballpark in June 1996. The truss, which is 517 feet long and 80 feet wide, supports the east side of the $333 million stadium's retractable roof. It was raised 172 feet to the top of the supports.

of this glorified past is that every child honed his skills in sandlots, but only a few did. Many had to work or were isolated from such activities. Today, kids have access to good equipment, smooth playing fields, and organized coaching. Between this, more leisure time in a rich country like America, improved training and diet, baseball has improved with a larger talent base that expansion accommodates. It probably will continue to accommodate it.

On March 9, 1995, Major League Baseball indeed decided that there was room for 25 more professional baseball players to entertain fans at the highest level of the game, in Phoenix, Arizona. They would have three years to prepare for their debut. Looking back now, with the hindsight of a decade, it is obvious that the plans and subsequent moves made by the Diamondbacks were far superior to those of the Tampa Bay Devil Rays, their expansion twins. One team has thrived. The other has withered.

TRIVIA

What political move first created an opportunity to bring Major League Baseball to Phoenix?

Answers to the trivia questions are on pages 159–160.

While Chase Field was being built on the outskirts of downtown Phoenix, the Diamondbacks were being developed through the expansion draft, the June free agent draft, the minor leagues, and at Phoenix Municipal Stadium, home of the Arizona Fall League.

The men who guided the team before they were a team were two well-respected baseball men who had built their reputations on the East Coast. Roland Hemond had built the great Orioles dynasty of 25 years earlier, three times earning the Executive of the Year award.

Manager Buck Showalter was more like an exiled prince, waiting for his loyalists to carry out the coup that would return him to power. Until he could manage a team in anger, he would have to oversee a growing minor league organization, from whence his club would emerge to sink or swim.

Showalter's previous big-league job was one of the most stressful in sports: manager of George Steinbrenner's New York Yankees. In that position, he developed a reputation as a workaholic and a winner. It was not enough. The Boss wanted world championships, which Showalter did not deliver. Thus was he let go in favor of Joe Torre. Today, the Yankees of the pre-Torre era are something out of the distant past, purged from the memory like failed apparatchiks of the Stalinist era.

While Hemond was the senior executive vice president of baseball operations, the club's general manager was Joe Garagiola Jr. Long before Randy Johnson or Curt Schilling were thrilling fans at Bank One Ballpark, Garagiola, Hemond, and Showalter, along with their staff, were "stars" of the Diamondbacks. There were also director of player development Mel Didier, director of scouting Don Mitchell, director of field operations Tommy Jones, and draft coordinator Ralph Nelson, in addition to a small army of medical, field, and scouting aides.

On November 18, 1997, these men were gathered at the Phoenix Symphony Hall Terrace for the expansion draft. Up until then, the team had been selecting amateurs. They mostly played for other organizations in the minor leagues, all under Showalter's, Garagiola's, Hemond's, Didier's, and Mitchell's watchful eyes. But today they would be drafting actual major leaguers or other hot prospects from other clubs. The draft was not a field day to get anybody. Each major league club had to submit a certain number of eligible players for the draft. There would be legitimate talent to choose from.

Overseeing it all: club owner Jerry Colangelo. He had arrived in the Valley of the Sun in 1968. Now he had brought big-league baseball to his adopted environs. Colangelo was willing to spend big bucks to bring a winner to the valley.

The day before the expansion draft, Colangelo inked shortstop Jay Bell, a former All-Star with Pittsburgh, for five years at $34 million. It upset many, who saw an "NBA-type mentality" creeping into baseball.

"As in most professional sports," Colangelo told *Sports Illustrated*, "there is a disparity between the haves and the have-nots. We hope to be one of the former. We have more debt than any expansion team in history, but we will spend if the opportunity is right, because we also expect to be a large revenue producer."

Still, Colangelo's high-spending ways reminded many of Florida Marlins' owner Wayne Huizenga. The billionaire founder of Blockbuster Video, Huizenga had built the best team money could buy. The mercenaries who made up his 1997 Marlins led them to the world championship and already were being dispersed to the four winds in a major sell-off.

The odd aspect of it all was that, because of Colangelo's money, the D'backs figured to be one of the six or eight highest-payroll clubs in baseball in 1998; yet small income teams like Oakland and Houston were "giving" them players.

"It's Robin Hood in reverse," Astros GM Gerry Hunsicker told *SI*.

The signing of Bell indicated that Colangelo hoped to build his team out of a certain kind of man. That kind of man would not be Charles Barkley, the loud-mouthed basketball star of the Phoenix Suns. It would also not be Barry Bonds, who, in 1997, told Colangelo, "When you get your team together, I'll be ready for you."

In an act that endeared Colangelo to millions of Arizonans, the D'backs owner said to Bonds, "I won't be ready for you," then got on an elevator, leaving the speechless Bonds in his wake.

On draft day, the D'backs (most were still calling them the DBs for short at this point) chose Brian Anderson, a fair pitcher who had seen World Series action with Cleveland in 1997. They also selected Cory Lidle, a control pitcher with the Mets.

DID YOU KNOW . . . That when Governor Rose Mofford signed Bill 1344, legislators surprised Representative Chris Herstam by presenting him with two baseballs? One was autographed by every member of the state house who had supported the measure. Every member of the senate who voted yes inscribed the other.

Man in the Middle

Jerry Colangelo's rebuffing of Barry Bonds is indicative of who he is. Colangelo is a man who means well. He legitimately tries to achieve things the right way. Being someone who has dealt in the upper corridors of power, business, and politics for many years, he has had to swim with the sharks, to be sure. He has made mistakes, but he has maintained his integrity as well as anybody who does what he does.

"I grew up on the South Side of Chicago in the 1940s and '50s in an area called Chicago Heights," he said. "The people there labored in the steel mills and in the factories. They were honest, hardworking people who took pride in their work and in their heritage. My family lived in the Italian neighborhood everybody called Hungry Hill. When you talked about your family on 'the Hill,' you were talking about the whole neighborhood. People respected one another. They took care of their own."

Colangelo went to work delivering newspapers twice a day to help his family. His old man was abusive. When Jerry became a teenager, he "threw him [his father] out of the house," according to Len Sherman in *Big League, Big Time*.

Colangelo was an outstanding athlete who turned down numerous professional baseball offers, choosing to play basketball at the University of Kansas. When Wilt Chamberlain left the Jayhawks early to play for the Harlem Globetrotters, Colangelo came home to the University of Illinois, where he made All-Big 10. He married his girlfriend, Joan, but did not make it to the NBA.

Colangelo went into the haberdashery business while playing semipro basketball on the side. Colangelo then went to work for a man named Dick Klein, who was a successful businessman with designs on owning a pro sports franchise. When Klein purchased the Chicago Bulls, Colangelo was his right-hand man. He did well in that position. In 1968 the expansion Phoenix Suns offered him the job of general manager. Colangelo decided to take the Suns job, in part because it was 20 degrees below zero when he departed Chicago's O'Hare Airport and 70 when he arrived in Phoenix.

The standard biographical profile reads like this: He came to Phoenix in 1968 with six suitcases, three kids, no car, no furniture, and less than $1,000 in his pocket.

Basketball was the last sport that seemed to make sense in Phoenix. Played indoors, it works against the great outdoor weather that makes baseball and football such a pleasant spectator activity.

The Phoenix ownership group did not live in the area. Colangelo was given the chance to run the Suns "his way." He put his stamp on the franchise, utilizing his own background as an all-conference collegian. He knew the game, but he also took to the marketing of the Suns.

In their first year, Phoenix made the playoffs, pushing the star-studded Los Angeles Lakers of Jerry West, Elgin Baylor, and Wilt Chamberlain to seven games. Over the years, Colangelo functioned as general manager, on occasion even handled coaching duties, and was the de facto owner of the team. He built the Suns from a sideshow into a major part of the community. They enjoyed success on the court and at the gate.

In the late 1980s, Colangelo turned lemons into lemonade. A drug and gambling scandal shadowed the Suns, almost costing Colangelo his job. He weathered the storm, but the Beverly Hills ownership group decided they had enough. They wanted to sell.

Several groups emerged as potential buyers. Colangelo had made a good living over the years, but had not accumulated the kind of money needed to buy a sports franchise. But he headed an investment group that successfully purchased the Suns. He was "first

DID YOU KNOW . . . That Jerry Colangelo played on a high school baseball team in Chicago Heights that also featured future Yankees and *Ball Four* author Jim Bouton?

*Diamondbacks owner Jerry Colangelo talks with reporters in September 1997
following three days of meetings among baseball owners in Atlanta.
Colangelo lobbied for his team to be placed in the National League West,
where he wanted to develop rivalries with the Colorado Rockies, Los Angeles
Dodgers, and San Diego Padres.*

among equals" within the ownership structure, a situation not
unlike the one Al Davis created for himself with the Oakland Raiders
in the 1960s.

Under Colangelo's leadership, the Suns moved up. Phoenix was
by this time a thriving sports market. The Sun Devils and Wildcats
joined the Pacific 10 Conference in 1978. The St. Louis Cardinals
football team moved to Arizona in 1989. The NHL, improbably,
entered the Phoenix market with the Coyotes. The Southwest was
the fastest-growing region in the nation. Many Californians were
moving to the state in order to avoid crime, smog, overcrowding, and
exorbitant home prices.

In 1992 Colangelo oversaw the completion of the fabulous
America West Arena. It was his savvy political leadership that

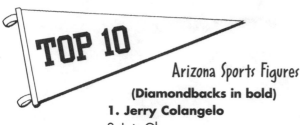

Arizona Sports Figures

(Diamondbacks in bold)

1. **Jerry Colangelo**
2. Lute Olson
3. Frank Kush
4. **Randy Johnson**
5. Charles Barkley
6. Del Webb
7. Paul Westphal
8. Jake Plummer
9. Bobby Winkles
10. **Curt Schilling**

created the public-private partnership necessary to build the basketball arena. It was considered the finest facility in the country.

As Len Sherman aptly points out in *Big League, Big Time*, the naming rights of America West Arena and the successful marriage of corporate sponsorships between the team, the city, and the business world in many ways started what became a major trend. Today, we see stadiums named after corporations, for better or worse.

In the case of Phoenix, it was definitely for better. In 25 years, Colangelo had turned the Suns from an expansion franchise, barely more than a minor league operation, to a cutting edge pro juggernaut—the very ideal for financial success in the athletic world. In so doing, he was an integral part of the growth of the NBA, which had ridden the Larry Bird–Magic Johnson 1980s to enormous popularity.

While all of this was happening, Los Angeles was experiencing some down years. The very nature of California politics shifted its power base from the south to the north. Orange County, a symbol of SoCal prestige, declared bankruptcy. New York was similarly faced with seemingly insurmountable problems. But Phoenix prospered and grew. Colangelo was the face of this growth, as demonstrated by his 1994 profile in *Forbes* magazine.

When baseball pursued expansion to Florida and Colorado in 1993, Colangelo was too busy dealing with America West Arena to get actively involved. But when MLB decided to pursue two more cities by 1998, Colangelo was approached as the man to head the Phoenix bid. A veritable who's who of businessmen and investors, in and outside the state, rallied to Colangelo. By now, everything he touched turned to gold. He was able to make a bid for the new franchise using mostly "other people's money" while retaining a majority share, just as he did with the basketball operation.

With a vote up for stadium funding, Colangelo was under the gun. He was also perturbed to discover that the other owners saw the purchase price of two expansion teams as a way to make up for lost profits from the 1994 players' strike. The price for the club skyrocketed to almost twice that of the $95 million paid for the Florida and Colorado franchises a few years earlier. Eventually, Colangelo was able to reduce the price to $130 million plus deferred TV revenue.

Then a controversy arose over a stadium tax assessed on the citizens of Maricopa County. Colangelo used all his powers to work out a deal, but not without engendering some public disenchantment. He was now more out front politically than he ever had been. He made mistakes a seasoned politician would avoid.

TRIVIA

Who was named Arizona's Most Influential Sports Figure of the 20th century?

Answers to the trivia questions are on pages 159–160.

Colangelo weathered that period just as he had the drug-and-gambling scandal of the 1980s but immediately found himself at odds with his new fellow owners, namely George Steinbrenner. Colangelo insisted that his team be placed in the National League West, refusing to consider any other possibility. He also signed several big-money free agents. He went after Buck Showalter and other former Yankees, a move Steinbrenner took exception to.

The building of Bank One Ballpark (now Chase Field), like any major undertaking, had its share of headaches, but when all was said and done, it was completed in time for the team's 1998 inauguration. Colangelo may have ruffled some feathers along the way, but he was a hero in Phoenix. He had created an arena and a major league stadium considered to be pure state-of-the-art. He had overseen a downtown renaissance that was responsible for numerous business expansions.

"Would I have gotten into this knowing what I do now?" he asked rhetorically in the first issue of the team's magazine in February 1998. "I'm not sure. But when they play the National Anthem with 49,000 fans standing in the ballpark—fathers, mothers, kids, grandparents—I know it will be worth it, and then some."

Laying the Groundwork

William Nathaniel "Buck" Showalter III will probably never be inducted into the Hall of Fame. Ultimate success, the brass ring, name the cliché; they have eluded Showalter. Nevertheless, it can be stated with some certainty that he laid the groundwork for two world championship clubs.

Showalter managed the 1995 Yankees into the playoffs for the first time in 14 years. His reputation within the game was as good as any manager in baseball. He was, in many ways, the "successor" of Gene Mauch, who was known for his brilliance and formidable work ethic. Showalter certainly was the kind of manager who left no stone unturned. Every conceivable edge that could be developed for his club was one he found and utilized.

Despite success in New York, George Steinbrenner fired him. Joe Torre inherited the team Showalter had painstakingly built. Torre deserves credit for winning the 1996 World Series, and for following that up with three more world championships in a row, from 1998 to 2000, but Showalter at the least deserves kudos for leaving Torre with a full cupboard to work with.

Perhaps even more credit is due Showalter for the work he did in building the D'backs, literally from scratch to a contender, which they were when he was fired after the 2000 season. It was Showalter's team that Bob Brenly, like Joe Torre in 1996, inherited and took to the Promised Land.

This leaves the inevitable question: did the Yankees and D'backs

TRIVIA

Who was voted the Diamondbacks' Rookie of the Year in 1998?

Answers to the trivia questions are on pages 159–160.

*Former New York Yankees manager Buck Showalter tries on his new uniform
during a news conference in Phoenix in November 1995, when he was named
the first manager of the Diamondbacks.*

win because of Showalter or because of his absence? If earnest hard
work, intensity, and commitment count for anything, the answer
would seem to be they won, at least in part, because of him.
Unfortunately, however, unless glory comes his way in the future, his
name will not reside among any of the all-time greats.

Showalter certainly found himself in a very unique position
between 1995 and 1998. He was the manager of a team that did not
yet exist for two entire baseball seasons. Colangelo snatched him
almost immediately after his '95 dismissal from the Yankees, where
he had toiled for 19 years.

Until the D'backs reported for spring training in 1998 and played
their first regular season game on March 31, Showalter could be
excused if he wondered whether his team was real or imaginary.

There was nothing imaginary about his years in New York,
where the Yankees manager lives in the ultimate reality show.

Showalter played seven years in the Yankees organization. In 1985, at the age of 28, he was named manager of their Class A farm club at Oneonta, New York.

Steinbrenner quickly learned of his work pattern. If there is anything that impresses the Boss, it is hard work; but of course it must result in victory in order to count for anything.

"He was the kind of manager who scouted *umpires*," *Sports Illustrated* wrote of Showalter. Like Mauch, Showalter was always tweaking his line-up or his strategy, looking for every possible edge.

Showalter quickly accomplished as a manager what he did not have the talent to accomplish as a player. He was fast-tracked up the Yankees ladder, a boy genius with blond hair and youthful good looks, in charge of the greatest dynasty in sports history. In 1994 Showalter was named American League Manager of the Year. In 1995 he returned the team to the postseason for the first time since they lost the 1981 World Series to Los Angeles.

His reward? A one-way ticket out of the Big Apple. *Don't mind the maggots.*

It was never explained, exactly. Showalter had just finished the third year of a three-year deal. The Boss may have added additional seasons dependent on Showalter firing several members of his coaching staff. To Showalter, the ultimate good quality was loyalty. He felt he could not live up to those principles if he fired some of the same people he had preached that ethic to. Worse yet, he felt the backbone of pinstriped tradition, going back to Babe Ruth and Lou Gehrig, had been loyalty. He was 39 and had a team on the verge of all-time greatness, but he stuck to his guns, accepting the axe instead of firing his coaches.

Showalter was out of work for about five minutes before the Diamondbacks snatched him faster than a hobo would a ham sandwich. Colangelo originally intended to wait, to hire the best manager available at the end of the 1997 season, but Showalter's availability changed all that. He was that highly thought of. While he publicly said he had landed on his feet, it had to be hard to go from the glamour of baseball's Roman Empire—Yankee Stadium—to the Arizona Fall League, which was his main domain in the next two years until the games started for real.

TOP 10

Managers Who Have Not Won a World Series
(Diamondbacks in bold)

1. Gene Mauch
2. Wilbert Robinson
3. Hughie Jennings
4. Charlie Dressen
5. Bill Rigney
6. Fred Hutchinson
7. Dusty Baker
8. Yogi Berra
9. **Buck Showalter**
10. John McNamara

"I respect the game so much," Showalter said. "I have a passion for it. It's something I grew up with. It's something you think you can hold your own in, and then you learn something new. You're always trying to get a little better. I learn something every day about baseball, about people."

When Showalter managed in New York, he kept his family in Pensacola, Florida, for two reasons: he could not be sure that he would stay on the job, and he did not want to subject his family to the pressures of New York. On the other hand, he immediately bought a home in Scottsdale—priced well below the outrageous tri-state real estate market of New York—when the D'backs hired him.

When Showalter took over as the Arizona manager, baseball was embarking on a major international kick. Subsequently, he found himself scouting players in Japan, the Dominican Republic, Canada, South Korea, and Mexico.

Showalter, a Southern gentleman, fit in perfectly with Colangelo's vision for the club. He said he did not want a player like Barry Bonds on his team. He openly criticized Charles Barkley, who was good but, "Did they win a world championship? That's the bottom line."

Showalter put forth a list of dos and don'ts for his club, involving cell phones, earrings, haircuts, uniform style, sunglasses, off-field attire, beards, and the like. By the mid-1990s, such rules would be hard to enforce. Perhaps only with an expansion team, which would consist of players often looking for second chances, could Colangelo and Showalter pull it off.

In the modern sports world, it was asking a lot. The average major league salary in 1997, the year before the club's debut, was $1.3 million. With that comes temptation.

Showalter did feel that some players who were "on the fence attitude-wise" could be brought in to the right clubhouse because "there's nothing stronger in our lives than peer pressure." The idea was to create a roster of players who "police themselves."

DID YOU KNOW . . . That Randy Johnson was named National League Pitcher of the Week twice in 1999? He earned the honor for his performances between May 24 and May 30, and again between August 16 and August 22.

Baseball Valley

The greater Phoenix area—specifically Scottsdale—is home to an enormous number of major league baseball players. The place with the largest number of players is Southern California, for several reasons. SoCal has a huge population. By far, the most players matriculate in the area's high schools and colleges. It's the home of three big-league teams, excellent year-round weather, and access to training facilities. It is a media capital, where players can pursue careers outside of the game.

But beyond L.A. and environs, the Valley of the Sun was an alluring place for pro baseball players long before the birth of the D'backs. Some 100 big leaguers live there, and about 300 ex-pros make it their residence, too. The reasons are not mysterious. First, many players are exposed to the area during spring training. They fall in love with it. The weather is, of course, terrific in the winter and during the spring training period. A player can work out in the off-season. Just like L.A., there are plenty of training facilities available. Many are not exposed to the summer heat because they are off playing in a different city by that time of year.

Baseball players like to party. They like beautiful women. There are numerous opportunities to party with beautiful women in Scottsdale, Arizona. This factor cannot be downgraded as a major reason why so many choose to live there.

Baseball players also tend to love golf. The courses in and around the resort town of Scottsdale are world-class.

The real estate values of the Phoenix area are a huge bonus, too. A home that would cost $1.5 million in Orange County might be purchased in Scottsdale or Mesa for $400,000. It is a safe, clean environment to raise kids, with good schools. The media is not intrusive in Phoenix. A man is allowed more privacy there than in New York or Boston.

The business of baseball has also made Phoenix/Scottsdale attractive. What with free agency and frequent trades, a player is less likely to buy a home in the city he plays in. Scottsdale offers a stable place to put down some roots, and of course it means being at home during spring training if the player's team is located in the Cactus League. By the late 1990s, this was more likely, with a number of teams moving to Arizona from Florida.

For all these reasons, the D'backs had an advantage before they ever played a game. Players with homes in the area all wanted to be a Diamondback when the time came.

Right off the bat, two superstars—Matt Williams and Randy Johnson—announced that they would be playing for Arizona when the time came. In addition to them, the team landed the best collegiate prospect in the country, Travis Lee of San Diego State.

Colangelo's willingness to spend money was quickly demonstrated by the $10 million signing bonus awarded to the 21-year-old Lee. Many a prospective free agent perked up and took notice of the money being handed out in the Valley of the Sun.

"I think it's insanity to pay that to an unproven college player," Kevin Malone, then the assistant general manager of the Baltimore Orioles (later the failed Dodgers GM) told the *L.A. Times*, "even though he's one of the highest-profile guys closest to being ready. It's another sign that the game's in trouble and another sign that the industry can't control spending....It's shocking."

Then-acting Commissioner Bud Selig said he, too, was "shocked."

Lee landed in the D'backs lap in a roundabout way that may or may not have been orchestrated by the Minnesota Twins. Minnesota selected Lee in the second round of the 1996 draft, but failed to offer

By the NUMBERS **44,449**—Average attendance at Chase Field in 1998 (seating capacity: 49,033).

The best college baseball player of his time, Travis Lee agreed to an eyebrow-raising $10 million deal with the Diamondbacks when he signed with the team in 1996.

him a formal contract, per MLB rules, within 15 days of the draft. They most likely did it on purpose, knowing they could not afford him.

The 6'3", 205-pound Lee was the winner of the Golden Spikes award, the Heisman Trophy of college baseball. He hit .416 playing first base for the U.S. national team, driving in 10 runs in nine games for the bronze medal–winning Americans at the Atlanta Olympics.

Lee was immediately assigned to the Arizona Instructional League. In 1997 he lit up the Class A California League with the High Desert Mavericks. D'backs player development executive Mel Didier called him "the best hitter I've ever seen."

Because the team did not have a Double-A team, Lee was loaned to the Milwaukee Brewers' Triple-A Tucson Toros. He became the first star, garnering the attention of Showalter, his staff, and Arizona fans before the big leaguers came to town.

In 1997 one of those big leaguers was toiling in Cleveland. Matt Williams came out of Carson City, Nevada, to make All-American at the University of Nevada–Las Vegas. Signed by the San Francisco Giants, he became an All-Star and fan favorite—a power hitter with a slick glove, a good attitude. He helped the Giants win the 1989 National League pennant, forming a powerful right-left combo with Barry Bonds. Then, General Manager Brian Sabean did the unthinkable—he traded Williams to Cleveland for some middle relief and a journeyman second baseman, Jeff Kent. Considered a terrible trade, it turned out to be a brilliant one. The players acquired turned the Giants into a contender again. Kent was named the Most Valuable Player in 2000. The Williams trade was viewed as the nexus for the club's great run, culminating in Bonds' four MVP awards and a 2002 World Series appearance.

TRIVIA

What names were considered before the team settled on Diamondbacks?

Answers to the trivia questions are on pages 159–160.

But Williams did not merely fade away. He at first made Sabean's trade look terrible when he enjoyed a 24-game hitting streak, powered 32 home runs with 105 runs batted in, earned his fourth Gold Glove at third base, and led the Indians to within one run of the 1997 world championship.

But there were other factors at play in Williams's life. His wife had left him and took their three children with her. Williams's ex-wife and kids lived in Scottsdale. Suddenly deprived of his family during the season, Williams stubbornly plugged away behind a veil of tears in Cleveland. His mind was on his children in Arizona. The birth of the D'backs, however, gave him hope.

That Devon White led Arizona in eight offensive categories in 1998?

At the 1997 All-Star Game, Williams told the *Arizona Republic*, "You can do anything at any time of the year here. You really can't beat it." Williams's commentary to the *Republic* was a job interview. He put his agent, Jeff Moorad, in charge of getting Colangelo and the Indians together to work out a deal. His performance made Moorad's job easy in terms of Williams's appeal to Arizona.

Cleveland knew he would be gone when his contract ran out, anyway. Arizona made a trade to acquire Detroit third baseman Travis Fryman. Moorad positioned Fryman as bait for the Indians. He was traded to Cleveland for Williams, without having played a game in Arizona. Williams met all of Colangelo's criteria for good citizenship. His desire to be near his kids outweighed his desire to play in the World Series, which to family-friendly fans was a plus.

Then there was Seattle's Randy "the Big Unit" Johnson, the most dominating pitcher in the game. He was also married, with a family and a home in the area.

"I've got two more years left here, and then I'm coming down, playing with the Diamondbacks," he boldly stated during spring training in 1996.

Showalter, however, was quick to discourage talk that, just because so many stars lived in the area, his club would become an all-star team. He realized that if Colangelo was going to collect all this high-priced talent, he would accumulate debt, making it difficult to run the organization. Besides, if a team could become a champion simply by signing all the homegrown stars when they became free agents, then the Dodgers and Angels would dominate baseball.

The Williams deal was notable not just because Cleveland cooperated with his request for a trade and the Diamondbacks traded talent to get Fryman in order to offer the Tribe something for Williams. It was notable because Williams was willing to play for $4.5 million in 1998. That was $2.5 million less than what was due him under terms of his Cleveland deal. His contract was structured with incentives to pay him more down the road as the club succeeded and made money to service their debt, creating a surplus. At least, that was the plan.

Williams's handling of his situation was in contrast to another star, Mark McGwire. In 1997 McGwire was traded by Oakland to St. Louis, becoming a free agent at the season's end. Like Williams, he was divorced and had a son living in Orange County. There is little doubt that, had he been willing to take less money like Williams, he could have worked out a deal with the Angels, Dodgers, or even Padres, allowing him to stay near his son. He went for Cardinals money instead, putting half a continent between himself and his kid.

Chase Field

Chase Field has the earmarks of a great stadium. When it comes to comfort, modern amenities, and clubhouse luxury, it has all the bells and whistles that define the newer stadiums that have been built since the 1980s. These include SkyDome, U.S. Cellular Field, Oriole Park at Camden Yards, Comerica Park, Jacobs Field, Miller Park, Ameriquest Field, Safeco Field, Turner Field, Citizens Bank Park, Cinergy Field, Minute Maid Park, Pro Player Stadium, PNC Park, Busch Stadium, AT&T Park, Coors Field, and Petco Park.

The one thing Chase Field lacks, however, is the kind of ambience that can only come from its surroundings. Dodger Stadium, a "shining city on a hill" overlooking a spectacular view of the gleaming downtown L.A. skyscrapers, has ambience.

Pac Bell Park, which begat SBC Park, which begat AT&T Park, sits on San Francisco Bay. Its fans get a view of the Bay Bridge, sailboat-dotted waters on one side, and the lights of the financial district high-rises on the other. It has ambience.

TRIVIA

Where do the Diamondbacks hold spring training?

Answers to the trivia questions are on pages 159–160.

Chase Field, on the other hand, was erected in a low-rent section, not far from downtown, a few blocks from the *Arizona Republic* building. It rises like the pyramids of Egypt out of the desert, a true world wonder, but its presence is its own reward. There are no waterfront vistas, no mountain spectacles, no Manhattan-style skylines.

Opened on March 31, 1998, under its original namesake, Bank One Ballpark (the BOB, for short), it has hosted the D'backs, the

TOP 10

Stadiums in Baseball

(Diamondbacks in bold)

1. AT&T Park
2. Dodger Stadium
3. Fenway Park
4. Oriole Park at Camden Yards
5. Jacobs Field
6. PNC Park
7. Safeco Field
8. Yankee Stadium
9. Petco Park
10. **Chase Field**

Insight Bowl, monster truck shows, conventions, concerts, and college basketball. It was originally named after one of the largest financial institutions in the U.S.

Officially, Chase Field is owned by Maricopa County and has a seating capacity of 49,033. It is the second of two pillars of downtown sports renaissance, the other being America West Arena, located a block west. The ballpark is bound by Jefferson on the north, 4th Street on the west, and 7th Street on the east. It is conveniently located, with easy access to Interstate 10 and I-17. It is 1,100 feet above sea level, a fact many do not know about Phoenix, Arizona.

Its designs are borrowed in part from the historic warehouse district surrounding the area. The former warehouse for the Stern Produce Building was incorporated into the south façade of the building. Fittingly, it now holds the ballpark's concession stands.

The decision to create a retractable roof was made in response to the age-old question of Arizona's summer heat. When closed, the games are played in pleasant, air-conditioned comfort. It is opened when the heat is not too intense, which generally occurs at the beginning and end of the season.

The decision whether to open or close the roof is always a hot discussion in Phoenix. A hotline was established for fans to call in and offer their two cent's worth. Sometimes in the summer, the clouds offer enough cover to justify opening the roof, especially for night games, but the indoor nature of the facility can create humidity.

The playing field consists of Bull's Eye Bermuda, considered the most suitable grass for retractable-roof facilities. In 1999, 135,000 square feet of the sod had to be replaced. As the grounds crew became more familiar with the turf, by 2000, only 8,100 square feet (94 percent less than the previous year) had to be replaced. In order to maintain needed photosynthesis, the roof remains open as long as possible to "feed" the grass, although there are sections of the field that receive incandescent growth lights as a substitute.

A dirt path between the pitcher's mound and home plate is a unique throwback to early stadiums. The 8,000-ton air-conditioning system could cool the equivalent of 2,500 typical homes in a state where such an amenity is *indispensable*. The fact is that the business

A fan's view from seat 1, row 32, in the right-field upper deck of Chase Field, shown in this photo taken before the park officially opened for the 1998 season.

DID YOU KNOW . . . The club's mascot is D. Baxter the Bobcat? D. Baxter was the brainchild of Jay Bell's son. He made his debut in 2000.

and political growth of the South and the West owes as much to the creation of air conditioning as any other factor. It's designed to bring temperatures down by 30 degrees within three hours, but cools only the seating areas, not every square inch of the ballpark.

Sightlines allow 80 percent of the seats to be within the foul poles, with no upper deck around the outfield. While Chase Field is used for football, it is a baseball stadium. In this respect, it is one of those newer stadiums built for our national pastime that creates, like Dodger Stadium, maximum fan comfort and game enjoyment. Dodger Stadium did this when many other stadiums in Atlanta, Philadelphia, Cincinnati, Pittsburgh, and other cities did not. Dodger Stadium continues to be a baseball monument, while those other stadiums have been replaced.

In a part of the country with eclectic tastes, the food at Chase reflects that. Nearly a quarter mile of concession stands include cafes and sports bars, offering the "pregame pub experience" with "postgame nightclub-style entertainment."

McDonald's, Little Caesar's Pizza, Blimpie, and Garcia's Mexican Food are among the concessionaires. Specialty ice creams, yogurts, smoothies, shaved ice, and popcorn are also available. In a rarity that makes sense since the citrus grower's warehouse is incorporated into the side of the stadium, fresh fruits and vegetables can be purchased.

Friday's Front Row Sports Grill is a popular hangout even when there are no games being played. It offers patio seating for D'backs games. The upper concourse features two Miller Lite beer gardens overlooking the field. The Arizona Baseball Club is located in right field on the Infiniti Diamond Level, providing fine dining, a spectacular view, and VIP luxury.

All things considered, Chase Field symbolizes all that is great about Phoenix. It is happening—a party atmosphere attractive to the young, the hip, and the single, but it is also a wonderful, family-friendly experience, featuring the best opportunity to enjoy the great game of baseball.

Joe Junior

Joe Garagiola Jr. has one of the most recognizable names in baseball. It is to his great credit that to a new generation of baseball fans, probably those born after 1975, it is his name they recognize. To older folks, it was his father, Joe Garagiola Sr., whose voice and personality evoked not just name-recognition but good memories.

Before Tommy Lasorda took on the job of baseball ambassador, Garagiola Sr. held that unofficial title. The elder Garagiola was a good-field, no-hit catcher for the Cardinals. He was behind the plate when St. Louis won the 1946 World Series. Garagiola was a childhood friend of Yogi Berra. They grew up together in the Italian Hill section of St. Louis. Garagiola's personality helped him become an NBC *Game of the Week* announcer and author of a best-selling, humorous baseball book. He was gregarious and popular, literally making a living telling Yogi stories for years with a series of sidekicks in the booth or on the sidelines.

Joe Jr. did not inherit his father's playing ability, and while he is by no means taciturn, he did not get the gift for funny talk, either. But he did get a first-class education, both formally and in the baseball sense. A cum laude graduate of Notre Dame, he went on to earn a law degree from Georgetown in 1975. He is a member of the Arizona, California, and New York Bar Associations.

But Garagiola was not a mercenary who came to Phoenix, taking over the club before moving on. Much of the club's success stems from its community roots; Colangelo, Garagiola, and others were Phoenix community leaders long before the team arrived. Garagiola indeed got his start through family connections, but his work as general counsel of the New York Yankees in the 1970s was based on his legal skills, not the perception that he knew baseball because of his old man.

After earning his spurs under George Steinbrenner, Garagiola moved to the Valley of the Sun in 1982. He specialized in the growing field of sports law for the firm Gallagher and Kennedy, becoming chairman of the Phoenix Metropolitan Sports Foundation from 1985 to 1987.

TRIVIA

Who did the Diamondbacks hire as their play-by-play broadcaster?

Answers to the trivia questions are on pages 159–160.

Before the D'backs came along, Garagiola worked for the Arizona Baseball Commission, whose work convinced MLB that Phoenix could support a team. It also helped to provide the vital demographics a bottom-line businessman like Jerry Colangelo needed in order to convince himself—and fellow investors—that such an undertaking had a realistic chance at success.

Garagiola became vice-chairman of the Governor's Cactus League Task Force, and was a member of the Mayor's Professional Baseball Committee. From there, he branched out to become chairman of the Maricopa County Sports Authority. When MLB awarded Phoenix a franchise in 1995, he joined the club.

As general manager, he made the key acquisitions that created the 2001 world champions. Using the many resources made available to him by the ownership prior to that season, he inked Mark Grace and Reggie Sanders, while also keeping Curt Schilling and Armando Reynoso in D'backs uniforms for an extended period. He avoided arbitration with closer Matt Mantei.

In 1998 the D'backs won a mere 65 games but turned that around to reach 100 in 1999. It was the greatest single-season turnaround in baseball history. The division title came six years sooner than any previous expansion franchise. Garagiola earned a third-place vote in the Executive of the Year balloting.

He signed key free agents, including Randy Johnson, Steve Finley, Todd Stottlemyre, Greg Swindell, and Greg Colbrunn. He picked up Luis Gonzalez and cash from Detroit for Karim Garcia. He brought in Tony Womack from Pittsburgh for minor leaguers. Womack immediately led the league in stolen bases for the third consecutive year.

His acquisition of Mantei, one of many good players Florida could not afford to keep in the wake of their 1997 World Series and fire sale, solidified the bullpen in the division title run of '99. The D'backs bullpen had the second-best ERA among National League relief corps.

He refused to unload Brian Anderson, who responded with effective pitching. He also oversaw the expansion draft, which produced six players on the roster at the beginning of the 2001 season, plus 10 others used to acquire the likes of Gonzalez, Womack, Schilling, and Matt Williams. His efforts at getting Williams were brilliant, involving a complicated draft of Detroit's Travis Fryman, who was then packaged to Cleveland for Williams when the third baseman desperately wanted to play in Arizona in order to be around his kids.

Eventually, Joe Sr. was brought on board as part of the D'backs announcing crew, a real treat and link to the game's past for Phoenix fans.

"My first involvement in baseball here came in the mid-'80s," Garagiola Jr. recalled. "I was part of an effort trying to save the Arizona Cactus League. The Cleveland Indians announced they were being aggressively courted by a number of places in Florida. And with only eight teams in the league, soon to be seven, it was a real wake-up call. We had a governor, Rose Mofford, who was a big baseball fan, and legislation was enacted that enabled us to solidify the league. It's gone from that point to us being able to attract the Chicago White Sox away from Florida. The Colorado Rockies also train in Tucson, with more clubs coming out here soon.

IF ONLY . . . Joe Garagiola Jr. had not decided, like so many fellow baseball people, to move to the Valley of the Sun in 1982, a big league team may never have come to Phoenix. Joe Jr. had no previous connections to Phoenix, having attended college at Notre Dame and Georgetown Law School, then working for the New York Yankees. When he decided to pursue a career in sports law, the Phoenix/Scottsdale area was a natural base, since so many players live there. Garagiola was pushing major league ball before Jerry Colangelo and is considered a major driving force in its coming to the state.

Joe Garagiola Jr. answers questions during a news conference in August 2005 after the Diamondbacks announced he had resigned from his longtime roles as the club's senior vice president and general manager to become senior vice president of baseball operations in the commissioner's office.

"The first time the idea of major league baseball was broached for Arizona came during the expansion process that produced the Rockies and the Florida Marlins. Arizona put together a proposal under Martin Stone, the owner of the Phoenix Firebirds, the Triple-A franchise. I was involved in my capacity with the Maricopa County Sports Authority. I pulled together a lot of information and resources on the public side. We went to New York and made a proposal to the expansion committee. Obviously, it was unsuccessful. In fact, we didn't even make the cut of the final cities that were considered. We did, however, get legislation on the books that if a major league franchise was granted to metropolitan Phoenix, the county Board of Supervisors could enact a sales tax to pay for a stadium."

In the early 1990s, San Francisco almost lost the Giants to Tampa Bay, spawning lawsuits that led MLB to mollify Tampa with another club, just as they had done for Seattle after the Pilots left for Milwaukee. Garagiola knew that if Tampa were to get an expansion franchise, it would need a second club to keep the league even. He went to Jerry Colangelo in 1993. Colangelo studied the issue at length before committing. When he did, he brought Garagiola in as a key founding member of the organization.

65–97

Because of the changing dynamics of baseball economics, the 1998 Arizona Diamondbacks entered their first season with higher expectations than any previous expansion team. The Florida Marlins, who entered the league in 1993, were the defending World Champions. Jerry Colangelo opened his pocketbook. Joe Garagiola Jr. made wise moves.

Unlike many previous expansion teams, this club would not have to play their first few seasons in a minor league stadium or rent from an established tenant. The 1961 Los Angeles Angels, for example, played first at the old Wrigley Field and then at Dodger Stadium.

It was felt that this was a club that might just contend in their first year.

It didn't happen. The D'backs were not as successful as that '61 Angels team. They drew large Cactus League crowds at home and on the "road" throughout March, when they were always the de facto home team in Arizona.

A sellout crowd of 49,198 turned out to see Arizona lose to the White Sox 3–0 in the final exhibition game—and first game ever played—at Bank One Ballpark. On Monday, March 31, 1998, the first regular-season game was played there. A host of notables, including Governor Rose Mofford, actor/investor Billy Crystal, Joe Garagiola Sr., Frank Robinson, and ex–Arizona State pitching ace Floyd Bannister, were part of the pregame festivities.

Jackie Robinson's widow, Sharon Robinson, was on hand for the retiring of her husband's number 42. The previous year, 1997, MLB retired that number for all times as part of the 50-year anniversary of his breaking the color barrier. The D'backs could not join that celebration at the time, but they could now. In a state that a decade earlier resisted the Martin Luther King Jr. holiday, it was a good sign.

The game was not: Colorado 9, Arizona 2.

In 1998 the club finished 65–97, good for fifth in the National League West Division. Businesswise, however, Jerry Colangelo hit the jackpot. More than three million (3,610,290, to be exact) fans entered Bank One Ballpark. The pool and Jacuzzi located in the outfield stands received a great deal of attention, especially from iconoclastic sportstalk host Jim Rome. Oddly, in a town filled with pretty girls, it was a photo of a pudgy dude in a swimsuit that made the national press, leading Rome to announce, "I don't need to see that."

The team's uniforms, designed in large part by Colangelo, did not receive rave reviews. They had so many different versions that it was hard to keep track. Colangelo, like Lakers owner Jack Kent Cooke years earlier, had a big thing for purple.

Twenty-three-year-old first baseman Travis Lee hit 22 home runs with 72 runs batted in and a .269 batting average. Third baseman Matt Williams hit 20 homers with 71 RBIs and a .267 average. Shortstop Jay Bell batted .251. Outfielder Devon White managed to hit .279 with 22 home runs and 82 runs batted in. He also stole 22 bases. Tony Batista hit 18 homers. Twenty-eight-year-old catcher Damian Miller was solid behind the plate.

Pitcher Andy Benes, a veteran fastball artist, was 14–13 with a 3.97 ERA. Brian Anderson was 12–13. Willie Blair, a 16-game winner in Detroit, was a disappointment, winning four against 15 defeats with a 5.34 ERA. Omar Daal had a nifty 2.88 ERA. Jeff Suppan was only 1–7.

Reliever Gregg Olson was effective, earning 30 saves on the strength of a 3.01 earned-run average. Overall, the club recorded a 4.64 ERA in a year dominated by offense.

DID YOU KNOW . . . That after the 1998 season, the club lost 9,000 season-ticket sales? This caused Colangelo to re-evaluate the timeframe for developing a winner from their short-term plan to "the time is now."

Andy Benes delivers the first pitch in the team's inaugural season to Mike Lansing of the Colorado Rockies. The Diamondbacks got off to a mediocre but promising start that first year.

Salary-wise, Benes was the team leader at $6,450,000, followed by Bernard Gilkey ($5,050,000), Jay Bell ($5 million), Matt Williams ($4.8 million) and Devon White ($3,510,000).

While the club's record was disappointing, there was much reason for optimism. Nineteen ninety-eight was the year Mark McGwire and Sammy Sosa supposedly "saved" baseball. In 1994 the players struck, destroying what had been a great season. Matt Williams, for instance, was on pace to break Roger Maris's single-season home-run record in 1994. The players walked out in the second week of August, never to return. There was no World Series, just October emptiness.

The Rockies and Marlins, both in their second year, had been successful up until that point. The strike halted their progress at just the wrong time. The Montreal Expos were in first place when the strike hit. Had the season played out and they had gone all the way—a distinct possibility—baseball might have been saved in Quebec instead of dying on the vine, as it eventually did over the next decade.

The strike hit well into the 1995 spring training, putting a big damper on baseball. A number of early-season games were canceled, meaning 1995 statistics were skewed.

It was under these circumstances that the D'backs entered major league baseball. They were hoping to overcome the strike. In building a beautiful stadium and organizing a team with some big names, they had done their part.

But in 1998 McGwire hit 70 home runs while Sosa slammed 66. Their neck-and-neck duel to overtake the Maris record renewed interest in the game. The Yankees also contributed, winning an incredible 114 games on their way to the world championship. The '98 Yankees are considered by many to be one of the two or three greatest teams ever assembled. They demonstrated that when New York is excited about baseball, it is good for baseball.

Colangelo, the competitor and former athlete, was not pleased with the 65-win season. He was aware of the fickle fate of fandom and knew that he was operating under a fairly narrow window of opportunity. He told Garagiola that the 3 million–plus fans who entered the ballpark in 1998 had done so out of curiosity and civic pride. Victory on the field—exciting teams, great players, big events—would be the driving force of his club's future. It would be the on-field success of the Arizona Diamondbacks that would have to separate them from what would become of the Tampa Bay Devil Rays.

By the NUMBERS **$354 million**—Construction costs for Chase Field.

Andy Benes

Born in 1967, Benes is one of those guys, like Jason Schmidt of the Giants, who seemingly has the ability of a star, yet whose results fall short of expectations. This is not to say he has not been an effective big-league pitcher.

The brother of another major leaguer, Alan Benes, Andy broke into the Show amid great expectations with San Diego. Prior to twirling in Arizona, Benes pitched for the Padres, Mariners, and Cardinals. He was an All-Star in 1993.

"Durable" and "consistent" replaced the hoped-for appellation "spectacular" as accurate descriptions of the hard-throwing right-hander. Mastering his slider proved elusive and his undoing. He posted 10 seasons of double-digit win totals, including a career best 18–10 for the 1996 NLCS champion St. Louis Cardinals. After making his name as a Padre over the first five years of his career, Benes spent his best two seasons in St. Louis before a contract dispute sent him to Arizona. Unlike most of Jerry Colangelo's picks, he did not materialize in Phoenix. Benes was returned to St. Louis in 2000 to spend the next two years pitching with decreasing effectiveness.

TRIVIA

Who was Arizona's ERA leader in 1998?

Answers to the trivia questions are on pages 159–160.

Benes broke in with San Diego in 1989. His 1993 All-Star year came with a 15–15 record. It was felt that he was a .500 pitcher because he was with bad teams, but ultimately he turned out to be...a .500 pitcher. He never struck out 200 batters in a year. In the strike-shortened 1994 season he led the league with 189 punch-outs.

In 1994 the Mets' Rico Brogna broke up his no-hit bid with a double in the eighth inning. The Padres won 7–0 as Benes fanned 13, walking only one in his one-hitter. He also drove home three runs with a double of his own.

After a brief stop in Seattle, Benes signed with the Cardinals as a free agent. In 1996 he started the year going 1–7, but evened his record at 8–8, beating the Reds 6–4. He then went on a 10-game winning streak. He had the best two years of his career. The club

Though he may have never hit the spectacular highs some had forecast for him, Andy Benes was a solid pitcher for the early Diamondbacks teams.

made playoff runs in 1996 and 1997. He bought a home there, announcing to the press he would finish his career as a Redbird.

Contract struggles ensued, probably because Benes and his agent figured his great potential would be reached, when it had not yet been reached (or ever would be). They figured he was owed for potential, a typical player's delusion from a class of people who assume the world owes them wealth whether it puts the payer in debt or not.

This attitude is based on the fact that that there too often are payers who will do just that. Enter Jerry Colangelo and his offer of a two-year, $12 million deal with the expansion Diamondbacks. On April 5, 1998, the Arizona Diamondbacks won their first game in franchise history, 3–2, over the Giants. Andy Benes got the win for the 1–5 D'backs.

Benes struggled in 1998 with a 3.97 ERA, so much so that despite his wealth he was deemed unworthy of a spot on the 1999 playoff roster.

By that time the cat was out of the bag: Benes was never going to achieve greatness. The third-year option on his contract was declined. Benes signed a new deal with the Cardinals in 2000. But age had slowed his fastball from its customary mid-90s velocity. Though he still accumulated 12 wins, his ERA was an unimpressive 4.88.

The 2001 campaign was even worse. His ERA soared above 7.00, and he failed to collect 10 wins for the first time since 1994. Benes's slow, straight fastball was meat for hungry bats. He became a frequent longball victim, becoming the 17th pitcher in major league history to give up four homers in an inning on July 23.

100 Wins

The performance of the 1999 D'backs was nothing less than incredible. It was an unprecedented effort, a second-year expansion team winning 100 games to capture the West. It was the result of owner Jerry Colangelo reacting to the changing marketplace of the game's economics. He knew that a new team and beautiful stadium would be a draw for a finite amount of time. Phoenix fans, he understood, were a savvy lot who wanted excellence on the field, and soon. They got it.

Jay Bell was fantastic. He hit .289 with 38 home runs and 112 RBIs to earn his $6.1 million salary. Third baseman Matt Williams ($8.1 million) was just as terrific. He batted .303 with 35 homers and 142 RBIs. Outfielder Luis Gonzalez emerged as a bona fide star with a .336 average, 26 long balls, and 111 RBIs. Center fielder Steve Finley was also outstanding, batting .264 with 34 homers and 103 RBIs to earn his $5,375,000. First baseman Travis Lee did not explode as many hoped he would. The former collegiate superstar batted only .237.

Tony Womack (.277) and catcher Damian Miller (.270) rounded out the offense. Other contributing members of the club included Kelly Stinnett, Bernard Gilkey, Erubiel Durazo, Hanley Frias, Tony Batista, Dave Dellucci, Lenny Harris, Rob Ryan, Dante Powell, Turner Ward, Rod Barajas, Ernie Young, Edwin Diaz, and Greg Colbrunn.

The strong offensive production was matched by excellent pitching, mostly in the form of Randy "the Big Unit" Johnson. He finally, after some maneuvering, lived up to his 1996 promise to become a Diamondback. He earned his $9.7 million salary, going 17–9 with a 2.48 ERA. Veteran right-hander Andy Benes went 13–12. Omar Daal was 16–9, and Armando Reynoso finished 10–6. Brian Anderson continued his effective work (8–2), and Todd Stottlemyre was 6–3.

Among many pleasant surprises in 1999, Luis Gonzalez had a 30-game hitting streak. Here he extends the streak to 22 games with a first-inning home run against New York Mets pitcher Rick Reed in May 1999.

In the bullpen, Matt Mantei earned 22 saves with a 2.79 ERA. Greg Swindell was 4–0 with a 2.51 ERA out of the set-up role, while veteran Gregg Olson still had something left in the tank, going 9–4 with 14 saves. Darren Holmes, Dan Plesac, Bobby Chouinard, Vladimir Nunez, John Frascatore, Byung-Hyun Kim, Erik Sabel, Amaury Telemaco, Dan Carlson, Ed Vosberg, and Vicente Padilla also contributed.

The season did not start out well, however. Arizona opened at Dodger Stadium, suffering a three-game sweep at the hands of Los Angeles. Next came a cross-country trip to Atlanta, where loss number four was hung on them by the Braves, 3–2. Randy Johnson finally reversed the trend with an 8–3 win over Tom Glavine.

By May 1, however, the club had righted the ship, improving their record to 14–11 with a 5–3 victory over Milwaukee at the old County Stadium. A seven-game winning streak closed out May after the D'backs defeated Montreal at Olympic Stadium 8–5 to up their record to 31–21. On June 2 the D'backs put on an offensive fireworks display, trouncing the hapless Expos 15–2.

On June 14 Johnson improved to 9–2 with a 2–0 win over Florida at Bank One Ballpark. A short three-game losing streak was snapped with a 9–5 win over St. Louis at Busch Stadium on July 2, when Arizona saw their record go to 44–36. They held their own on the Cardinals' turf in the mid-summer heat, perhaps establishing for the first time to the baseball world that the club was for real.

Korean reliever Byung-Hyun Kim attracted a fair amount of attention. Ever since he first appeared in spring training, his side-winding submarine style seemed to portend greatness. At first, he looked unhittable, but eventually his fastball began to flatten out, however.

A five-game winning streak culminated with a 4–2 win over L.A. at Dodger Stadium. Randy Johnson's 11th win on the final day of July elevated the club to a 59–46 mark.

The Giants visited Phoenix, losing two of three to the ascendant second-year club. Arizona was the talk of baseball. The dog days of August did not stop them: five wins in a row in Chicago and Philly. Johnson's 12th victory came over the Cubs at home, giving his team a 68–51 record.

With the Big Unit leading the way, the Diamondbacks finished August at 79–54. They held their own at Atlanta, then put on a stretch run with seven straight wins, beating Colorado 9–3 at home to go to 97–60. On the last Sunday of the season, Anderson's 10–3 win over San Diego lifted the club to 100 victories.

TRIVIA

How many hits did Luis Gonzalez have in 1999?

Answers to the trivia questions are on pages 159–160.

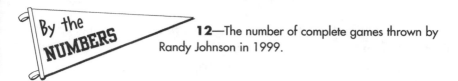

12—The number of complete games thrown by Randy Johnson in 1999.

Johnson won the Cy Young Award. Steve Finley earned a Gold Glove. Tony Womack won the Lou Brock Award for leading the senior circuit in stolen bases. Matt Williams was voted the club's Player of the Year by the Arizona chapter of the Baseball Writers Association of America. Good guy Luis Gonzalez was appropriately awarded the Good Guy trophy.

Williams was the NL April Player of the Month, Johnson the Pitcher of the Month in July. Jay Bell, Williams, Finley, and Johnson (twice) earned league Player of the Week honors in 1999.

The club was 52–29 at the BOB, 48–33 on the road, winning the division by 14 games while drawing an astounding 3,019,654 fans to their games at home. The team ERA was 3.77, their batting average .277 with 216 long balls.

With so much success, the Diamondbacks allowed themselves to dream big dreams come October. Their first-round opponents were the veteran New York Mets, who qualified for the wild card after a playoff win over Cincinnati. With home-field advantage, the Diamondbacks might have overlooked New York. Unlike 1998, when the Yankees looked impregnable, in 1999 the brass ring was there for whoever had what it took to grab it. Randy Johnson was roughed up in an 8–4 loss, immediately swinging momentum to the Mets. Todd Stottlemyre rode the bat of Steve Finley to a clutch 7–1 win in the second game, sending the teams to Shea Stadium with a split.

Whether the raucous Shea crowd got to them is not fully explained, but Arizona fell flat in two straight losses, ending this fabulous season with disappointment. Omar Daal was ineffective in a 9–2 defeat. The last game ended when New York's Todd Pratt hit a tenth-inning home run to clinch the victory.

Ultimately, Atlanta captured the National League pennant. In typical Yankees form, the Bronx Bombers rebounded from a sub-par regular season, got hot in the playoffs, and beat the Braves to take their second straight world title; their third in four years.

The Bell Curve

Jay Bell was born in 1965.

"I grew up all over the world," said Bell. "My dad was in the air force, but we settled down in Pensacola, Florida, and the team that I ended up choosing to watch was the Los Angeles Dodgers with Garvey and Lopes and Russell and Cey. They were clean-cut, All-American guys. Tommy [Lasorda] preached the 'Dodger Blue' stuff, and I kinda fell for that. I enjoyed that group of guys. Steve Garvey was my favorite player growing up, and they were an exciting team to watch, especially in '77 and '78."

Bell came to Arizona after having played in the Twins, Indians, Pirates, and Royals organizations since 1986. His best previous success was in Pittsburgh, where he was a member of Jim Leyland's teams that fell just short in excruciating playoff losses to Cincinnati and, especially, Atlanta.

Bell earned the 1993 Gold Glove, the same year he made the All-Star team. In 1999 he joined teammates Matt Williams, Randy Johnson, and Luis Gonzalez in a memorable All-Star Game at Boston's Fenway Park. It was made especially exciting in a pregame ceremony featuring Red Sox legend Ted Williams, who was surrounded by a phalanx of admiring All-Stars, led by San Diego's Tony Gwynn.

Bell signed a five-year, $34 million deal with Arizona before the club's inaugural 1998 season. It was a risky move by owner Jerry Colangelo, who obviously had yet to make a dime. Bell became baseball's highest-paid middle infielder, but it was his good reputation as a team leader that made him so attractive. If the pressure was on him, Bell did not show it. He hit a career-high 38 homers while racking up 112 RBIs and 132 runs scored in 1999.

That only six franchises in baseball history have gone by the name of states instead of cities? These include Minnesota, California, Texas, Colorado, Arizona, and Florida. California originally was named after Los Angeles, later named after Anaheim, and is again named after L.A. New York's teams are named after the city, not the state, although there is implied double meaning. The Arizona Cardinals football team chose to represent the whole state, too.

Bell was a first-round pick of the Twins in 1984. He made 129 errors over his first three minor-league seasons. In 1985 he was traded to the Indians in a deal bringing starter Bert Blyleven to Minnesota. He reached the Show in 1986, ironically facing Blyleven in his first at-bat. Bell hit the first pitch he saw for a home run.

Jay was traded to Pittsburgh in 1989, where he became an every-day player. In 1990 he assumed the job of starting shortstop, maintaining the position of fan favorite in the Steel City for seven years. He was a linchpin of Jim Leyland's strong defensive clubs, which captured the National League East for three straight years.

Bell began as a line-drive hitter. He hit 16 home runs in 1991 and improved defensively. In 1993, with the great Barry Bonds having departed for San Francisco, Bell scored 102 runs, batted .310, and stole 16 bases.

With Bonds gone, the club suffered on the field and at the gate. Bell was traded to Kansas City in December 1996. He had success when he hit .291 with 21 home runs and 92 RBIs. Bell became a sought-after free agent after the 1997 season, which was when Colangelo made his big move. Bell was impressed by everything he saw in Arizona, but what influenced his decision the most was the opportunity to play for D'Backs manager Buck Showalter, whom he had known since his high school days in Florida.

The first year was below par: a .251 average with 20 homers on an expansion team. But Bell was the linchpin of the 1999 NL West champions. Bell switched to second base at the end of 1998 and stayed there. Bell slammed 36 of his 38 circuit blasts from his new position, a total exceeded only by Rogers Hornsby, Davey Johnson, and Ryne Sandberg among second baseman. His sixth-inning grand slam off Oakland hurler Jimmy Haynes in the final game before the

All-Star break won $1 million for an Arizona fan who correctly predicted the batter and the inning for a bases-loaded blast.

In Bell's third year, his offensive production fell: .267 with 18 home runs and 68 RBIs.

In the 2001 World Series, Bell came to bat against Yankees closer Mariano Rivera with runners on first and second with no outs. He laid down a bunt, but Rivera was able to get to it, making the force throw at third base.

"I think any time you're in that situation, certainly there are some negative thoughts that come into play, even though the objective is to make sure you maintain a positive frame of mind," he said. "In my situation I had first and second with no outs, laid down a bunt, and Rivera got off the mound quickly, made the throw to third base, and I'm runnin' down to first base thinking, 'Shoot, I just screwed up the World Series!' Yet at the same time I know who's coming up behind me. Tony [Womack], Counce [Craig Counsell], and Gonzo [Luis Gonzalez] had very successful seasons. Certainly

ALL-DECADE TEAM

1990s All–Decade Diamondbacks Team

Position	Name
Pitcher	Andy Benes
Pitcher	Randy Johnson
Pitcher	Brian Anderson
Pitcher	Matt Mantei
Catcher	Damian Miller
First Base	Travis Lee
Second Base	Jay Bell
Third Base	Matt Williams
Shortstop	Andy Fox
Outfield	Luis Gonzalez
Outfield	Devon White
Outfield	Tony Womack
Manager	Buck Showalter

Jay Bell rounds the bases after hitting what proved to be a game-winning home run against the Florida Marlins in August 1999.

there was a very comfortable and confident feeling with those guys coming up. That was how it happened all season long. Whenever one player failed, the next guy picked him up. Tony certainly came through in the clutch and then Gonzo did as well, so it was a very exciting finish." Gonzalez's hit won the game.

It was Bell's first world championship; redemption after three playoff losses in Pittsburgh.

"It was an extraordinary accomplishment to have the opportunity to score the winning run after 16 seasons of trying to win a World Series," he said. "Rarely does anybody have that opportunity. The last two times any team has won in their last at-bats, I scored the winning run last year [2001], and then in 1997 Craig Counsell scored the winning run for the Marlins. It's certainly a very, very memorable moment. Each and every team has a desire to get to the World Series and win. That's the objective every year coming out of spring training: to produce as a team and allow yourself that opportunity. The way our season went last year, we felt very good and very sure about ourselves. Throughout the course of that seven-game Series, some exciting baseball was played. It went right down to that seventh game and the last inning. To put two runs up against a team like the Yankees and, more specifically, a pitcher like Rivera, was a very, very exciting feat."

Matty

Born in 1965, Matt Williams came up as a shortstop by trade. He came from Carson City, the capitol of Nevada. Located about half an hour from Lake Tahoe to the west and Reno to the north, Carson City is a small town known for gambling and legalized prostitution. It is also known for excellent youth league baseball.

A tight-knit community, Carson City has well-organized kids leagues, top-notch facilities, a strong high school program, and a nationally known American Legion team called the Carson Capitols. Every Fourth of July, the Capitols host a tournament that draws the best summer baseball teams from the West.

Williams was weaned in this atmosphere of baseball nirvana, earning a scholarship to play for coach Fred Dallimore (whose son Brian later played in San Francisco) at the University of Nevada–Las Vegas. In the 1980s UNLV was a major collegiate baseball power. Williams earned All-America honors before getting drafted by the Giants.

Williams's favorite team was the Dodgers because the local TV station televised an L.A. game once a week, but for all practical purposes the Reno-Carson-Tahoe area is considered to be an extension of the San Francisco Bay Area, located a few hours west down Interstate 80. Numerous Bay Area residents make vacation homes in the Tahoe area, trekking to Reno for gambling and other vices.

Beginning in 1987, Williams established himself as a favorite with the Candlestick Park faithful. It looked great at first, with San Francisco capturing the 1987 division crown before losing in seven games to St. Louis in the NLCS. In the 1989 earthquake World Series, Oakland swept the Giants in four games.

That Matt Williams was one of 11 players to hit 300 home runs in the 1990s?

Williams was a star in San Francisco—an athletic third baseman, a dangerous slugger, and a team leader. With a reputation for hard work and a good attitude on the field, Williams was also known as a family man, seemingly in a great marriage. Like many players, he bought a home in Scottsdale, where the Giants trained in the spring. Life seemed just right.

While Bonds's reputation has always been shaky, he nevertheless possessed the kind of star quality that the workmanlike Williams did not have. Despite Williams's strong performance, the team fell after the 1989 championship year, and with it, fan interest at dilapidated Candlestick Park dropped precipitously. In 1992 it appeared the team was headed to Tampa Bay.

First a committee headed by sports agent Leigh Steinberg was formed to save the club. An ownership group led by Safeway magnate Peter Magowan came on board to buy the team. They kept it in the city, vowing to build a new stadium, and most importantly, signing Pittsburgh free agent Barry Bonds.

In 1993 everything came together. Fans who would not come to Candlestick if they were paid to do so came in droves to see Bonds, a two-time MVP in Pittsburgh. He had his best season up to that time, winning a third MVP in 1993.

The revival of the team, the fan interest, the new ownership commitment, and the presence of Bonds in the lineup were just the spark Williams needed. He took his career to a new level. In 1993 he helped spearhead a club that won 103 games but lost a playoff bid on the season's last day when Atlanta won and San Francisco lost at Dodger Stadium. In 1994 Williams's 37 homers in August had people talking about Roger Maris' 1961 record of 61. That all went down the tubes when the players struck, depriving fans of records, an exciting finish, and, of course, a World Series.

A consistent .270 hitter with home-run power to all fields, Williams spent 10 seasons in San Francisco.

Matt Williams connects for a grand slam, driving in Danny Bautista, Luis Gonzalez, and Reggie Sanders in a game against the Dodgers in September 2001.

"If there's one thing I learned here, it's never take your eyes off the ball," Williams told a reporter from the *San Francisco Chronicle*, with regards to the swirling winds at the old Candlestick Park.

His 1997 trade to Cleveland dismayed Giants fans, but it turned San Francisco around. Some journeyman pitchers and infielder Jeff Kent came to them. After several sub-par years, the Giants became contenders from 1997 to 2004.

Williams's performance in Cleveland was remarkable because of his well-documented break-up with his wife, leaving him forced to live without his kids. The kids flew to Cleveland when the Indians were at home, but anybody who understands the baseball routine knows this is not conducive to quality time. His children eventually hated the long plane flights.

Many baseball players would have brooded or gone on a strip club rampage; either way letting their problems disrupt their performance on the field. Williams stayed focused. It was his leadership that helped Cleveland get to Game 7 of the 1997 World Series before losing to Florida.

The creation of the D'backs—Joe Garagiola Jr.'s ability to orchestrate a complicated trade, Colangelo's willingness to pay him, and Williams's willingness to defer his contract—all added up to what seemed to be a gift from God when Williams found himself playing in Arizona. He was now in the same town where his children lived.

In 1999 Williams had 142 runs batted in, demonstrating power over and above his previous seasons. Teammates such as Bell and Gonzalez also showed such strength. After 1999 Williams suffered a series of unexplained injuries, including sore hamstrings, hip flexor problems, and a bizarre, arthritis-like ailment. He recovered, and by May of 2001 was hitting well. However, he was unable to make full use of his legs, hitting only 16 home runs in 106 games.

During the 2001 season, Williams got into a heated argument with Giants manager Dusty Baker over his perceived intentional beaning by reliever Chad Zerbe. Williams and Baker were close friends. They quickly decided to make nice.

TRIVIA

Matt Williams has dabbled in acting. What show did he appear on?

Answers to the trivia questions are on pages 159-160.

Leo Durocher once said, "Nice guys finish last." He was wrong. Williams was a nice guy who, in 2001, finished first when his club captured the Series from the Yankees. It was vindication for the decisions he made, namely orchestrating a trade to Phoenix for the express and noble purpose of being a better father.

Gonzo

The BALCO steriod scandal uncovered dirty secrets not just in our national pastime, but throughout sports. The unfortunate aftermath of this has been that virtually all players who displayed unusual power numbers, mainly in the late 1990s and early 2000s, are under suspicion of drug abuse.

Luis Gonzalez falls under suspicion because his home-run numbers exploded. There is no proof, no investigation swirling around him, but thanks to Bonds, Jose Canseco, Ken Caminiti, Sammy Sosa, Mark McGwire, Rafael Palmeiro, and a host of others, *all successful baseball players* live under a cloud of suspicion. If it is true many of these players injected themselves with performance-enhancing drugs, then the fault lies with them, too, whether the public possesses knowledge of it or not. This includes Gonzalez, Brady Anderson, Randy Johnson, Roger Clemens...the list goes on and on. There are some players who, common sense says, never took anything. There are many unable to benefit from the common sense test for reasons obvious to anybody with access to the known facts.

So why have Gonzo, Johnson, even Clemens, avoided the scrutiny that other players like Barry Bonds have had to endure? For several reasons: there is no proof, in part because baseball does not want the embarrassment a true investigation might reveal. The friendly demeanor of Gonzo and the sense of upfront straightforwardness seen in Johnson have helped exempt them from the scrutiny paid to others, especially the loudmouths, racists, philanderers, and moral unimpressives.

Gonzo came up, seemingly an average ballplayer of slight build, with Houston, the Chicago Cubs, Detroit, and then Arizona.

That Luis Gonzalez and his wife, Christine, had triplets (Megan, Jacob, and Alyssa) born in 1998? The joy and inspiration that comes from fatherhood must not be overlooked when considering its impact on his on-field performance.

He blossomed in the 'Zona desert, making the 1999 and 2001 All-Star Games. In Detroit, Gonzalez was a .267 contact hitter. Playing in a home-run park, he sprayed line drives.

In December 1998 he was traded to the D'backs for Karim Garcia. His performance once in Arizona resembled a man approached by somebody who said, "Take this, it will magically make you better." He took, and it magically made him better. If Gonzo did it naturally, then an apology is owed him, but frankly the apology is not owed from people who have used logic and facts to make a reasonable hypothesis; the apology is due from those who created the problem in the first place. Those people are *baseball players who take steroids*, therefore creating a not-unreasonable suspicion that *many baseball players take steroids!*

Prior to the trade, Karim Garcia and Luis Gonzalez seemed interchangeable baseball talents. After the trade, Gonzalez did things that Hall of Famers like Jimmie Foxx and Hank Greenberg used to do. Karim Garcia continued to play like Karim Garcia. Gonzo was a decent outfielder, but lacked a great arm. He turned 32 in 1999.

He was thin in high school, where he played second base. He led off in a lineup that included prep All-American and future Yankees star Tino Martinez. Drafted by Houston, Gonzalez broke into the major leagues in 1990. Playing in the Astrodome, there was little incentive to become a power threat, since the heavy indoor air made that a futile effort.

Gonzalez was traded to the Cubs in June of 1995, but before he could much contemplate changing his hitting approach to accommodate batter-friendly Wrigley Field, he was returned to Houston in 1997. Despite not achieving stardom or longevity in Chicago, he did achieve popularity. The "bleacher bums" signed a ball for him and threw it to him at the end of his last game there. It remained a prized possession. Even though he was from Florida, Gonzalez signed with

Luis Gonzalez watches his 13th home run of April during the 2001 season, when he tied the major league record for the most home runs in the first month of the season.

Detroit in 1998 to be near his sister, who lived in Michigan. Hitting at Tiger Stadium, a relative launching pad over the years, he began strength training, adding 10 pounds to his 6'2" frame.

One day during batting practice, teammate Bobby Higginson told him, "'You gotta learn to hook the ball to play in this park to take advantage of the short porch in right." He opened his stance and started pulling the ball, hitting a career-high 23 homers.

The trade to Arizona was a major coup by general manager Joe Garagiola Jr. At first, manager Buck Showalter considered using Gonzalez as a lead-off hitter, but he had Tony Womack to fill that role. Gonzo was platooned with Bernard Gilkey in the number three slot, between Jay Bell and Williams. Gilkey did not materialize, but Gonzalez, sandwiched between the likes of Bell and Williams having career seasons, saw incredible pitches to hit.

His season started with a 30-game hitting streak, followed immediately by a 12-game streak. Gonzalez batted .390 throughout much of the first half of the season. He finished the 100-win year with a .336 average, 36 points better than anything in his career.

The argument that Gonzo did things naturally has its merit. His change of stance in Detroit benefited him. He developed confidence probably lacking before, a factor any athlete can attest is beyond measure. Getting pitches to hit between two sluggers while hitting from a power slot, instead of lead-off, made a huge difference.

Bernard Gilkey? He went to join Karim Garcia in the Hall of Mediocrity.

Gonzalez's smile, media-friendly attitude, and genuineness with everybody attracted the fans. On a team that Colangelo actively wanted to represent strong values, he fit right in. Because he was so unheralded prior to 1999, he was left off the All-Star ballot. Arizona fans and a local radio station organized a huge write-in campaign. He received 40,000 online votes, many from kiosks set up around town. It did not get him elected to the starting lineup, but it did help him make the team as a reserve.

On the strength of his All-Star popularity, the Diamondbacks decided Gonzo deserved not to be paid singles hitter money but home-run-hitter money; namely $12.5 over three years. He delivered as promised and then some while maintaining a .300-plus batting average. Despite his rapid success in his first two years in Phoenix, Gonzalez's performance in 2001 ranks among the all-time top five in terms of sheer improvement over previous records.

Batting stances, lively balls, good pitch selection, thin air, short porches, and weight-lifting do not adequately explain what happened. He started on fire with 13 April home runs, a league record not previously accomplished by Hank Aaron, Willie Mays, Barry Bonds, Sammy Sosa, Mark McGwire, Frank Robinson, Ralph Kiner, Mel Ott, or any other human being who has ever played in the National League since 1876.

As Ronald Reagan once famously said, "You ain't seen nothin' yet." By the end of July Luis Gonzalez had 40 *home runs!* The all-time record had been set three years earlier by Mark McGwire, whose body had noticeably grown. Sammy Sosa, once a fairly thin kid from the Dominican Republic who now looked like an NFL linebacker, and McGwire broke the old records...several times. They made it look as if Roger Maris, who lost his hair hitting 61 in '61, had been below standards. In 2001 Gonzalez threatened McGwire and Sosa. McGwire's body, in particular, seemed to fail him in 2001. Sosa was also into a downward slide that included revelations that he corked his bat.

"Meet the new boss, same as the old boss," The Who once sang in the rock anthem "Won't Get Fooled Again," but baseball was fooled big time in 2001, by Barry Lamar Bonds. He made McGwire and Sosa look like pikers with his 73 longballs, but for a long time little old Luis Gonzalez matched him tater for tater. As Slim Pickens might have said, "What in the wide, wide world of sports is goin' on here?"

TRIVIA

Where did Luis Gonzalez play college baseball?

Answers to the trivia questions are on pages 159–160.

In August and September, Gonzalez cooled down, finishing with a mere 57. That of course is three less than Babe Ruth's best, and is one less than Foxx and Greenberg; not to mention better than Ted Williams, Harmon Killebrew, Ernie Banks, or anybody else whose plaque could be hit by a man throwing darts blindfolded inside a certain building in Cooperstown, New York.

Through it all, Gonzalez maintained his wonderful demeanor, impressing people with a photographic memory for names and faces. He remembered everyone he met at all the ballparks—players,

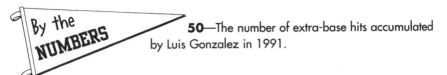

50—The number of extra-base hits accumulated by Luis Gonzalez in 1991.

umpires, stadium personnel. He established a reputation as the highest tipper in baseball. He took pride in breaking a worker's "record" for biggest tip of the year. Rookies benefited from his generosity as he picked up tabs and dinner checks. His attitude toward people was 100 percent democratic. They all got his good side.

Steve Finley

Born in 1965, outfielder Steve Finley graduated from Paducah (Kentucky) Tilgham High School, then received a degree in physiology from Southern Illinois University–Carbondale, a program with a long, successful baseball tradition in the Midwest.

Finley was accepted to the chiropractic school at Logan College in St. Louis, but professional baseball intervened. Drafted 11th by Atlanta in 1986, he chose to stay in school, earning All–Missouri Valley Conference honors twice. He was a third-team '86 All-American and played on two conference champs.

In 1986 Finley was a member of Team USA. They earned a bronze medal in the Netherlands. Both of his parents were educators back in Kentucky.

He came up with Baltimore in 1989. Finley played for Houston and was a key player on contending San Diego teams in the mid-1990s before coming over to the Diamondbacks. He made the All-Star team in 1997 and 2000 and earned Gold Gloves in 1995, 1996, 1999, and 2000.

Finley was an excellent athlete, but it was his smarts and baseball instincts that gave him a better jump on the ball than others with more speed. His competitive nature has been the driving force of his success, although his hustle led to occasional small injuries.

In 1996 Finley teamed with Ken Caminiti to lead San Diego to the playoffs, hitting 30 home runs with 95 runs batted in. He hit 28 in 1997. He had never hit more than 11 prior to '96.

On September 28, 1999, he hit two homers against the Padres while suffering from a bulging disc in his back. Finley was one of those line-drive hitters who suddenly became sluggers in the late

Steve Finley makes yet another great defensive play as he catches a fly ball hit by the New York Yankees' Tino Martinez in Game 3 of the 2001 World Series.

1990s. He enjoyed two consecutive 30-plus homer seasons while maintaining a high on-base percentage.

He contributed 34 homers with 103 RBIs in the 100-win 1999 season, and followed that up with 35 longballs in 2000.

In the world championship 2001 season, with others stepping up production, he moved runners along, drew walks, and was part of a team offensive concept that worked well.

"The one thing about this team," he said of the clubhouse humor in Phoenix, "is that there's nobody immune to the abuse and punishment. I don't mean that in a bad way. I mean that in a fun way. Everybody's always gettin' ripped. This team checks their egos at the door, and if you misstep a little bit, you know you're gonna get busted for it and take the brunt of everybody's punishment."

Before coming to Phoenix, Finley was a fan favorite in San Diego during his four years there. He helped them to the 1998 World Series, but San Diego had spent too much money to get there. Finley, Kevin Brown, and Greg Vaughn left as free agents. Colangelo identified Finley as the kind of personality who would fit in with his family atmosphere in Arizona. In an example of fans rewarding goodness and identifying unimpressive behavior, Finley was cheered upon his return to Qualcomm Stadium. Kevin Brown, a great talent but not a great guy, was jeered. He received ovations during each at-bat, despite collecting three RBIs against his old team.

Finley won the 1997 Chairman's Award with San Diego for his efforts within the community. He inspired the Padres Scholars in 1995. Steve and his wife, Amy, have four children and live in the San Diego area.

"My wife gave birth to our fourth child, a little girl," Finley said of the birth of his daughter. The Finleys' fourth daughter was born on September 10, 2001. "I went home that night and got the call at about 6:30 in the morning from my sister-in-law. I turned on the news but I waited a while to call my wife. I didn't want to tell her because she'd just had a baby the night before—ya know, the excitement of that coming to the downer of this. It was one of those days that you just don't know how to feel as you watch it."

They are active in giving back. The Finleys inspired a program to buy 20 tickets per game for underprivileged youth. When they moved on to Arizona, they transferred the program to Chase Field. Finley and his wife toured Indonesia and post-communist Hungary in the 1990s, conducting baseball clinics and donating equipment. The Steve Finley Foundation was formed to encourage kids to stay in school, earn a degree, and live drug-free. A country-western

DID YOU KNOW . . . That in 2004, Steve Finley homered in the ninth inning of the last game of the season to give Los Angeles an improbable comeback win over San Francisco, propelling the Dodgers to the West Division championship?

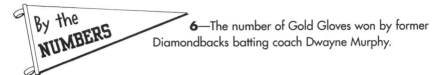

6—The number of Gold Gloves won by former Diamondbacks batting coach Dwayne Murphy.

aficionado, Finley has worked with singing legend Garth Brooks, who is a big baseball fan, to create the "Touch 'em All" division of the Teammates for Kids Foundation.

Finley made $5.3 million in 2001 and has become a multimillionaire playing the game. He later starred for the Dodgers, helping them win the 2004 West Division title, but he has always maintained the small-town values he grew up with in Kentucky.

"I felt in spring training we had a real good chance to win it all," he told Bob Page in *Tales From the Diamondback Dugout* of the 2001 title team. "We looked around the clubhouse and we had Schilling and Johnson leading the rotation—just a whole host of arms. Our offense and defense [were] gonna be great. We had every ingredient it takes to win the World Series. Let's just go out there and do our jobs. I think what got us through the season and into the playoffs was not looking ahead. We weren't thinking that we were playing the Pittsburgh Pirates or the San Francisco Giants. We were worrying about the game we were playing that day, not concentrating on anything else, and I think that's what gets you where you need to be."

Finley appears to be one of those guys Colangelo acquired who totally refutes the Leo Durocher maxim about "nice guys finishing last." He worked hard, fit in with the team, and sacrificed when called to do so. He has been a favorite with fans and the community every place he has been. Like many of his teammates, fatherhood and marriage inspired him to be a better player—a surefire sign of good character.

It is to Colangelo's and Garagiola's credit that they were able to identify, like good college football recruiters, guys with character and also ability. Putting those qualities together is not as easy as it would seem. Many athletes are stars on the field, lowlifes off it.

Big Unit Was a Bay Area Boy of Summer

On June 11, 1999, this author (then the lead columnist for *Street-Zebra* magazine in L.A.) had the opportunity to speak with an old USC classmate, Arizona Diamondbacks southpaw Randy Johnson, at Edison International Field of Anaheim.

The Big Unit recalled playing for an amateur summer team in the Bay Area, Bercovich Furniture. A mutual bud of ours from 'SC, Tony "Bruno" Caravalho, always talked about his days with that club, so I was spurred to ask Randy about it. The legendary Rod Dedeaux recruited the pitcher after he struck out 21 of 22 batters while pitching for Bercovich (he also threw a perfect game in high school).

"Dedeaux was larger than life," recalled Johnson. "He was getting on in years by the time I got to 'SC, though."

Johnson still stayed in touch with Trojans teammate Mark McGwire. What did he think of the fact that the two most dominant players in baseball went to the same college?

"It's a testament to the history of that program," he stated. Did he still root for Troy? "Sure."

Two years later, I met up with Johnson again, this time at Chase Field (still known then as Bank One Ballpark). I was in town on assignment with the *San Francisco Examiner* as their lead sports columnist. Johnson's size and accomplishments made him the Paul Bunyan of baseball. In the modern day version of David and Goliath, he was Goliath. This guy was not Everyman. He was to pitching what Rommel was to desert combat, Chuck Yeager to aviation, Einstein to quantum theory.

Randy Johnson's natural skills made him stand out above and beyond the normal, the average, and the humdrum.

Still, this Frankenstein of baseball, this 6′10″ millionaire *wunderkind* who was so different, so skilled, so gifted, was in fact very much like the rest of us.

The Chair

Even though it had been only two years since I last saw Randy Johnson, and I attended USC with him, I approached him with the question, "Do you remember me?"

It has been my experience that some famous sports stars are so busy, isolated, adored, or self-consumed that people once in their wedding parties are not recognized upon approach. In the case of Mark McGwire, another 'SC classmate of ours who was actually more a college friend of mine than Johnson, I had to remind him who I was during a 2001 Pac Bell Park interview. He seemed irritated to be bothered.

I inquired of Craig Stevenson, McGwire's USC roommate and the best man at his wedding.

"That's just not part of my life anymore," he sniffed. Stevenson, his best man, revealed that he had to go through his agent to get in touch with McGwire. 'SC teammate Randy Robertson, who played little league ball with Big Mac in Pomona, California, acknowledged a similar experience. Ex-teammate Terry Marks, now in charge of all Coca-Cola's North American operations, went through elaborations to secure a signed ball from his former teammate for his son. He was rebuffed.

I mentioned various other Trojans teammates. No interest was offered.

Dear God.

When I approached Johnson in the D'backs locker room and asked if *he* still remembered me, the reaction was completely different.

"Of course I do," he said, and gave me a hearty smile and a handshake.

"Do you have a few minutes?"

"Of course I do."

Johnson had a comfortable recliner next to his locker at Chase Field, but he was not sitting in it.

"Do you mind if I sit here?" I inquired.

He nodded, "Sure," so I did.

Apparently, the recliner was not available to just anybody. Pitcher Mike Morgan dropped by, opened a nearby refrigerator, and offered me a beer.

"No, thanks," I said. Gee, what a nice guy.

"Can I get you a sandwich?" asked Matt Williams.

Wait a minute! I was getting goofed on by the Diamondbacks.

"I'm not supposed to be sitting in your chair, am I?" I ask him. He smiled.

"You know what?" he said. "Us Trojans stick together. You can sit anywhere you like."

You gotta love the good ol' boy network. I conducted the interview, which lasted the better part of 45 minutes, sitting in the recliner. It eventually got so comfortable, I almost told Morgan I had reconsidered that offer of a cold brew.

The conversation centered not on Johnson's great career statistics, or "what is it like to be Randy Johnson?" which seems to be the semi-boring focus of 99 percent of modern-day sports interviews. At least not the Randy Johnson we saw on TV. No, it was time to take a trip down memory lane, to the Big Unit's roots in the Bay Area. Since I was writing for a San Francisco paper, this was appropriate. The subject was Bercovich Furniture, the summer team he played on as a teenager, to be explored in full detail.

Bercovich Furniture

When the punditocracy of baseball talks about a guy's background, they often refer to the high school he played at. High school baseball is very much a rite of passage, as American as apple pie. However, it may not be the place where a baseball player best hones his budding skills. The prep season usually starts when the weather is colder, wetter. The season goes about 30 games, give or take. Outside interests like school, girls, friends, and cliques can encroach on one's concentration.

Summer ball is where progress is made. It can be American Legion, Connie Mack, Joe DiMaggio, or Senior Babe Ruth League. Kids play more games than during the high school season. They travel, face great competition, and the team itself often draws from a

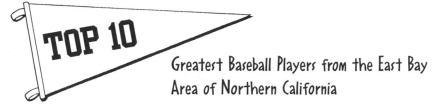

TOP 10

Greatest Baseball Players from the East Bay Area of Northern California

(Diamondbacks in bold)
1. Frank Robinson
2. Rickey Henderson
3. Willie Stargell
4. Joe Morgan
5. **Randy Johnson**
6. Dennis Eckersley
7. Vada Pinson
8. Billy Martin
9. Dave Stewart
10. Jimmy Rollins
HONORABLE MENTION: Chris Speir, Claudell Washington, Mark Davis, Dontrelle Willis.

larger population base than the school, making for an "area all-star" concept.

The weather is warm. The players have fewer distractions in the summer. They are more skilled by August than they were in March.

Years ago, there was a team in Baltimore called Mama Leone's. The sponsor was, as you can guess, an Italian restaurant. Reggie Jackson played for Leone's. *Sports Illustrated* wrote an article about them. Today, a top prospect might play for a travel team.

In the 1970s and '80s, such a team played hard, fast baseball at Laney College in Oakland, on dusty ball fields from one end of the San Francisco Bay Area to the other—and beyond. They were called Bercovich Furniture. If that name sounds familiar, it is because Mr. Bercovich, who ran a furniture store (and maybe a few other things), was a close, personal friend of Raiders' owner Al Davis. Whenever talk would break out about new stadium financing, or a reshuffling of the ownership group, Bercovich's name would pop up. You never saw his picture. He was not a media dude, but he was a mover and a shaker.

Maybe he owned some land, or had some parking lots that could be converted into the Raiders' new football palace. Whatever. He had money, he loved sports, and he was connected to the powers-that-be.

He also liked to see young athletes prosper.

Bercovich had the dough. Ray Luce, who ran Bercovich Furniture's team for years, knew the game and had passion for it. Often, the team played doubleheaders, but in different cities—maybe an afternoon game at Laney, then a nightcap in Walnut Creek. Heck, they played *triple-headers*. Between Memorial Day and Labor Day, Luce's team might have played 120 games.

TRIVIA

When did Mike Morgan, a member of the 2001 Diamondbacks, make his big-league debut?

Answers to the trivia questions are on pages 159–160.

Luce loved baseball and kids. He liked to be around them. The guys who played for him swore by him. One of those guys was a very tall, thin southpaw who had been born in Walnut Creek and was pitching at Livermore High School.

"Yeah, we'd play three games a day," recalled Johnson. "We'd play in Hayward, we'd play in Oakland. We'd play wherever there was a game and a team to play against. It was a Bay Area all-star team. Jack Del Rio played for us. Don Wakamatsu, Doug Henry, Kevin Maas. We had guys from Berkeley. Guys would travel to play or move in from outside the area."

Wakamatsu and Henry were stars at Tennyson High in Hayward and went on to star at Arizona State. Henry, of course, was a top relief pitcher for years, including productive seasons with the Giants. Del Rio starred in baseball, basketball, and football at Hayward High before leading Southern Cal to a 1985 Rose Bowl victory. He played linebacker for the Minnesota Vikings and became the head coach of the Jacksonville Jaguars.

Maas, from Oakland's Bishop O'Dowd High School, played at the University of California and, for a couple of seasons at Yankee Stadium in the early 1990s, looked like the next Babe Ruth.

"It was the best team I've ever been on," said Johnson, obviously making this reference within context. "The caliber of ball was excellent, and it was a lot of fun."

Another Bay Area left-hander, Bill "Spaceman" Lee, once made a similar statement when he said the best team he ever saw was "either the 1968 USC Trojans or any Taiwan little league team." Space did concede that the 1975 Cincinnati Reds could compete in this league, as well.

"Luce would have us travel all over the Bay Area," said Johnson, "and beyond the Bay Area. We'd go to the Wine Country, the Central Valley, anywhere. My dad would often drive me. It was a bit of a haul, but Dad would take me to the games. I really appreciate my dad. He played mostly rec league softball, but he saw that I had potential ability.

"Luce was mostly a good organizer. He wasn't the greatest manager I ever played for, but there's no doubt he knew how to put a good team together."

Livermore: Cy Young Capitol

Livermore, California, is a place known mostly for its laboratory, where nuclear weapons are worked on by government scientists. Other than that, it is just down the road from Altamont, where the Rolling Stones held their infamous free concert in 1970, which resulted in a Hell's Angel stabbing a fan.

Today, it has become a bedroom community. A train system called BART makes it easier for its residents to commute to San Francisco or Oakland.

"It was a small town," recalled Johnson. "At least, it seemed like a small town. It's 40,000 or 50,000, but it's a place where you are removed from city life. It was pretty rural."

The Big Unit was more of a farm boy type, not a sophisticate from the San Francisco Bay Area. He reflected what Livermore was all about. Still, little old Livermore has produced more Cy Young Awards (six) than any town in America. Sure, Johnson has five, but Mark Davis, a left-hander out of Granada High, won one at San Diego in 1989.

"I never thought about that," said Johnson. "I remember when Davis was at Granada, that was a few years before me, and I'd go to see him pitch."

Johnson went 4–4 at Livermore High in 1982, but the Cowboys did not give him much support. His 1.65 ERA and 121 strikeouts in

66⅓ innings pitched in 1982 landed him All-East Bay Athletic League and All-County honors. Atlanta made him their fourth-round draft choice.

You hear about these players who turn down millions of George Steinbrenner's or Ted Turner's dollars to play college ball at USC or Stanford. This must have been the case for Randy, right?

"Johnson was not the best pitcher on the team," said Bruno Caravalho, who also played ball at USC. He was referring to Johnson with both Bercovich and at Southern California.

"I Thought He Was Kind of Wacky"

Johnson discussed his future with his dad. They both knew that he was a work in progress, a project. Heck, this guy was the Hoover Damn. The Tennessee Valley Authority. The Pyramids.

Minor league baseball might have eaten him alive. It was decided that the University of Southern California, a national powerhouse led by the greatest collegiate coach of all times, Raoul "Rod" Dedeaux, would be the best place for him to hone not just his diamond skills but his life skills, too. USC came through with the scholarship, and that was where Mr. Johnson went next.

Dedeaux, winner of 11 national championships, was to his sport what John Wooden was to his. This guy was a genius, right? He must be a coach who combined the discipline of Vince Lombardi, the tact of Mike Krzyzewski, and the strategic thinking of...Napoleon.

"I thought he was kind of wacky," said Randy.

Some guys just hang on too long, and that seemed to have been Rod's case, but in his prime, there were none sharper.

"He was the best baseball man I ever played for," said Bill Lee, who starred at USC 15 years before Johnson arrived. "He didn't look like a ballplayer, but he had eyes in the back of his head. He knew every play that would happen before it happened. He was in the seventh inning when the game was in the third."

"He was the sharpest tack in the box," said Dedeaux's successor, Mike Gillespie.

"Rod never really was on hand," said Johnson of the Dedeaux he played for. "[Assistant coach] Keith Brown ran the program. I mean, he surrounded himself with good baseball people and he was a fun

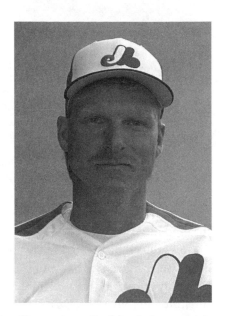

Randy Johnson, a Northern California native and former USC star, broke into the majors with the Expos as a 25-year-old.

guy who I enjoyed playing for. I still run into Rod in L.A., and it's always nice to see him."

After playing a couple years of minor league ball, I was finishing up my degree at USC during the period when Johnson and McGwire were playing there. I was even a volunteer JV coach for a while. While Dedeaux was at the top of his game during Spaceman Lee's era, he was pushing retirement during our time. Dedeaux, a millionaire trucking executive who "moonlighted" as 'SC's coach for a dollar a year out of love, had never been a full-time collegiate coach. By the 1980s, he was showing up for games late, sometimes after attending a cocktail party. Dedeaux retired after the 1986 season and passed away watching USC lose on TV to Texas in the 2006 Rose Bowl.

Despite Dedeaux's absenteeism, the Trojans had one of the most talented college baseball teams ever assembled with Johnson and McGwire. In the entire history of this great game, it can be argued that the most intimidating offensive player ever was McGwire, and the most intimidating pitcher was Johnson. So, naturally, facing mere college opponents wearing uniforms that read "UCLA," "Arizona State," and "Fresno State," these two larger-than-life diamond gods led Troy to unheard of heights of glory, right?

Actually, they lost in the NCAA Regionals—when they even made the playoffs.

"I wished I'd learned more," Johnson says of his college career (1983–1985). "I was still a project when I left."

The Project was also a lefty. A California lefty. The connotations of what this means go back a long way. Rodeo, California's Lefty Gomez, aside from being a Hall of Famer with the Yankees, was known as "El Goofy."

Spaceman was, well, Spaceman...the King of Flaky Lefties.

It was hard to pin Johnson down, but Dedeaux, a familiar figure at 'SC, Dodgers, and College World Series games until his passing, recalled him this way: "Randy was one of the most colorful personalities in college baseball. But he also had the ability to go along with it. He was an excellent competitor, and had a major league fastball. He always provided an exciting performance."

Johnson may not have been Mark Fidrych or even Turk Wendell, but he was a team cheerleader who attracted attention on the hill. He talked to himself, frequently ran around the infield shouting encouragement to teammates, and congratulated himself for good pitches.

Big Mac was all he was cracked up to be—a two-time All-American, College Player of the Year in 1984, and an Olympian. It was not just Mac and the Unit, either. Del Rio was a catcher on those teams, a good ballplayer. Pitcher Sid Akins was an Olympian. Brad Brink would pitch in the big leagues. Randy Robertson and Mickey Meister were talented, hard-throwing right-handers. Phil Smith and lefty Bob Gunnarsson were tough pitchers. Even the pitching coach, Bill Bordley, had pitched in the majors and had once been considered the best college pitcher ever (Bordley

DID YOU KNOW . . . That while Erubiel Durazo is a native of Hermosillo, Mexico, he came to Tucson, Arizona, as a youth, attending Amphitheater High School and Pima Community College? Ex-NFL and USC great Rikki Ellison also went to Amphitheater. Durazo returned to Mexico undrafted, playing for the Monterrey Sultans, who had a working agreement with the D'backs. Durazo signed with Arizona prior to the 1999 season.

became a Secret Service agent who was assigned the Chelsea Clinton detail at Stanford). Aside from McGwire, 'SC had offense in the form of third baseman Craig Stevenson, spray-hitting outfielder Alby Silvera, and power threats Reggie Montgomery and John Wallace.

With all this talent at his disposal, Dedeaux could not get his club into the NCAAs in 1983. They were blown out in the regionals the next two seasons. After going 5–0 as a freshman, Johnson was statistically mediocre in 1984 and '85. This reflected his team's enigmatic performance.

"I never gave that much thought to the fact that Mac and I were teammates," said Johnson in 2001, "and now we're so-called 'dominant' players. He's a home-run threat now, and he was then. He has size and ability.

"The fact we didn't get into the College World Series was disappointing. You need pitching. We had talented pitchers—Akins, Brinks, Meister, Gunnarsson—but we didn't pitch well in the regionals. We were not as outstanding as you have to be to win at that level. Pitching wins games. I had height and ability, but I was a long way from where I am now."

A Rapport with Other Power Pitchers

Johnson's professional career is well documented. He pitched for Montreal and came into his own in Seattle. He dominated the game in a way few pitchers ever have. He also had a connection with power pitchers of previous eras.

"I talk to Tom Seaver when the Mets come to town," said Johnson. Seaver starred at USC before becoming a superstar with the Mets, and later a TV sportscaster in New York.

"I talked to Nolan Ryan a few times. I have rapport with guys like that. They have the same make-up that I do. As a pitcher, if you have the ability to talk to guys who've been there before you, that's just great. I've seen Sandy Koufax a few times, too, and admire him because his career has some parallels to mine."

Another Trojan lefty, Barry Zito, hit the scene in 2000–2001 with the sudden impact not of the "project" Johnson, but more reminiscent of the 21-year-old Vida Blue. The young pitcher who interested

Johnson more because of the parallel was St. Louis's hard-throwing Rick Ankiel.

"He's proven that he's a fine pitcher," said Johnson. "He pitched great until the postseason. It's nothing that can't be worked on."

The Cardinals were patient with Ankiel, but it never did work out for him. Not everybody was so patient with Johnson when he was pitching at Jamestown, West Palm Beach, and Jacksonville. After going 0–4 at Montreal in 1989, the Expos decided he was expendable.

If they had been more patient, like the Dodgers were with Koufax, they could have reaped the benefits of having one of the game's greatest pitchers starring for them.

Still, hindsight is always 20/20. Johnson entered his zone and stayed there a long time. To paraphrase Glenn Campbell, "By the time he got to Phoenix," he was happily married. He raised his family in Paradise Valley when playing for the D'backs, not far from Chase Field. He was low-key and thoughtful in that 2001 interview, which became a full two-page spread in the *San Francisco Examiner*.

He might even let you sit in his chair. If he does, make sure you tell his teammates that you only drink imported beer.

Wandering in the Desert

The 2000 Arizona Diamondbacks were like Moses' Hebrew tribes. Having won a great battle, they found themselves wandering in the desert, ultimate victory still so close, yet so far away.

It was a season of trial for an overconfident team that won 100 games the previous season. In the millennium year, a third-year club that shattered the record for all second-year expansion teams posted an 85–77 record. The third place D'backs failed to make the playoffs, which the third-year Rockies had done in 1995.

It was not a failed team, however. Had they overextended, played beyond their talents in 1999? In 2000 first baseman Greg Colbrunn batted .313. Jay Bell was an offensive disappointment, dropping to 18 homers and a .267 average. Shortstop Tony Womack had another fruitful season, batting .271, but his stolen-base production dropped from 72 to 45. Third baseman Matt Williams also disappointed with a mere 12 homers, but the outfield combo of Luis Gonzalez and Steve Finley was outstanding again.

Gonzo hit .311 with 31 home runs and 114 RBIs. Finley slammed 35 homers with 96 runs batted in. Danny Bautista was creditable (.317), while catcher Damian Miller played solid defense.

Travis Lee had people worried. The former Golden Spikes award winner lost his regular job, responding

TRIVIA

Former D'backs pitcher Greg Swindell set a number of University of Texas records, including for single-season strikeouts (204), single-season wins (19), and career strikeouts (501). What NCAA record did he set?

Answers to the trivia questions are on pages 159–160.

Jay Bell reacts to a call by umpire Dana DeMuth as Seattle's Mark McLemore calls for time after stealing second base in a July 2000 game. The Diamondbacks had a letdown after the successful 1999 campaign.

with a withering .232 average and no power. Bernard Gilkey faded into the woodwork (.110), and Rod Barajas had yet to mature as a player.

A look at the pitching staff is to look at a mystery. At first glance it would seem they were again strong; not the 1973 Oakland A's, perhaps, but by the juiced-ball, small-park, 'roided-up era of the 2000s, pretty good.

First there was Johnson, who collected $13,350,000. If one uses moral relativism to justify such things, it could be said he came as close to "earning" that kind of unreal money as any player in the game. He was 19–7 with a 2.64 ERA, and was considered the most dominant pitcher in baseball. Brian Anderson (11–7), Armando Reynoso (11–12), and Todd Stottlemyre (9–6) did what second-tier pitchers are expected to do: they pitched five or six innings and kept their team in the game.

Perhaps the key to unlocking the mystery comes in the form of Mr. Curt Schilling. Schilling came up to the league relatively unheralded. Whereas the 6'10" flamethrower Johnson was called the Big Unit and compared to Nolan Ryan, there was little in Schilling's high school or minor league record to suggest greatness.

He achieved success in Philadelphia, but by 2000 he was on a familiar precipice between almost-greatness and washed up. His mid-season trade to the Diamondbacks came with high hopes. His pedestrian 5–6 record, 3.69 ERA, and $5,650,000 salary made him look like just another overpaid baseball man. His mediocrity goes a long way toward explaining the team's 85-win doldrums. In succeeding years, he has been nothing less than heroic. A legend in two cities.

How do you explain that?

Matt Mantei's 4.57 ERA and low 17-save total probably tells much about the 2000 season. Byung-Hyun Kim officially confirmed that he was not unhittable; perhaps he made this point too clearly (6–6, 4.46). Mike Morgan, who it is rumored broke in on the same team as Christy Mathewson, was reliable in his usual reliable way.

Arizona defeated Philadelphia in the opener at Chase Field 6–4 behind Johnson. Their 3–0 start was encouraging; more of the same. A 16–9 April looked to be par for the course. They played excellent ball in May, and by mid-July, when Johnson (15–2) beat St. Louis 3–2 at Chase to up their record to 55–41, all seemed well.

But in San Francisco, to quote Steven Stills, "something is happening here." What it was became increasingly clear. Ever since the Matt Williams trade of 1997, the Giants had been like proverbial Israel; the underdog that keeps on winning.

The Giants had beaten back a better Dodgers team in 1997, wiping away the last vestiges of the O'Malley mystique. The Dogs

DID YOU KNOW . . . That the 2001 world championship was the third ring won by Diamondbacks pitcher Todd Stottlemyre? He pitched for the 1992 and 1993 World Series–winning Toronto Blue Jays.

looked like the old studio system trying to hang on with musicals when the public wanted sex and violence. The brutal handover to News Corporation was their version of Heaven's Gate. The hiring of Kevin Malone, the signing of Kevin Brown—L.A. could not airbrush their faults. The Giants emerged as a winner, their rival not in LaLa Land but in 'Zona.

In 2000 they moved into Pac Bell Park, suddenly the nicest stadium in baseball. The changeover from the abominable Candlestick, in congruence with the emergence of the power-hitting Jeff Kent and the resurgent Barry Bonds, was a shock to the system. In 2000 the D'backs kept waiting for Frisco to fade away, but like another old soldier, they had an Inchon up their sleeves.

On July 26 the Diamondbacks lost their fourth straight, 8–4 at St. Louis. The Giants, with Kent and Bonds battling each other for clubhouse alpha male supremacy and, on the field, for the Most Valuable Player award, picked it up. Playing in foggy San Francisco, they were spared the kind of summer heat that Arizona, retractable roof or not, must suffer through. Schilling never lived up to his promise. The season slipped away.

A sweep at the hands of Los Angeles in September allowed the Dodgers to nip them for second place behind the 97–65 Giants, who, after all their success, seemingly gave the playoff series to the Mets away. Their supposedly all-knowing manager, Dusty Baker, made several bad moves in defeat.

That Championship Season

The 2001 D'backs may not have been prohibitive favorites to capture the National League West, but they were by no means underdogs. In many ways, they were perfectly positioned. They were a veteran ballclub and had a roster of successful, tested big-league players, some of whom were already stars.

They had experienced terrific success in the form of a 100-win season in 1999, but any overconfidence afflicting them was tempered first by the playoff loss that year followed by a disappointing 85–77 2000 season.

The first major question was: are they getting old fast? This is the bugaboo of great teams. When does it happen? How does a GM get ahead of the curve? Atlanta had successfully avoided wholesale old age for years, utilizing a formula that strangely worked regular season after season, always with October disappointment. The Yankees, especially in the 1950s, used trades and the farm system to replenish the old with the young, enjoying good results.

Branch Rickey and a host of subsequent executives said the secret was to trade a player one year early instead of a year too late, but that can backfire. Case in point: Frank Robinson, considered an "old 30," was traded to Baltimore in 1966, where he led the Orioles to four pennants.

Would Johnson, Bell, Finley, Williams, and company get old sooner or later? That was the first question. The second question revolved around Curt Schilling. The Phoenix native was a successful major league pitcher. He had been in pro baseball since 1988. He was an All-Star, a winner, a competitor. He was not a dominant pitcher. He had been expected to help the club down the stretch in 2000.

He had not. Who was Curt Schilling? At the very best, the Diamondbacks were hoping for something close to his 15–6, 3.54 performance with Philadelphia in 1999. The year he led the Phillies to the World Series in 1993, his ERA was 4.02. He was a guy who needed run support. If he got it, the club was hoping for something like 14–10, 3.65. He had put up enormous strikeout numbers in recent years, indicating either improvement in his fastball or better control, but there was no expectation that he would give them a Cooperstown-worthy performance. In the spring of 2001, anybody who mentioned Schilling as a Hall of Famer would be laughed at. Schilling was better than a journeyman, but not expected to be a Cy Young candidate. Nobody mistook him for Bob Gibson circa 1967–1968.

Finally, the second major question: will this veteran team respond to the loose Bob Brenly better than they had to the disciplinarian Buck Showalter? Showalter was the perfect father figure to take an expansion team, teaching them to be winners. He was not a modern manager in the sense that multimillionaires with top big-league resumes—which the Diamondbacks were by now—needed a guy telling them not to wear their hats backward and to shave, trim their sideburns, and tuck in their shirts. The "high school Harry" rules of 1998 fit Colangelo's vision of the perfect team, but in a way the owner and the general manager had set the manager up for failure. They had found the kind of upright guys who did not need discipline.

Then there was first baseman Mark Grace. One of baseball's best hitters with the Chicago Cubs throughout the 1990s, Grace signed as a free agent in December for $3 million. He was an eccentric without the All-American image his first few years, but he was by no means a bad guy. He fit into the clubhouse, perhaps creating just that touch of levity needed. He also performed to his usual high standards: .298 with 15 homers and 78 RBIs. He was still one of the game's best glovemen around the bag.

The 2001 Diamondbacks did not match the 100 victories of '99, but their 92–70 mark was good enough for first place in the NL West. Bell did not reach the power numbers he had displayed a few seasons earlier, but on a good team his .248 average and strong defense at second base was just the ticket. Shortstop Tony Womack again provided speed—a catalyst for "little ball" when needed. Third baseman Matt Williams was now making $9 million. He had signed for less, giving the team a chance to win, to draw fans, and create revenue. He had contributed to their accomplishing just that, and now reaped the rewards. Like Bell, he did not match power numbers of the past, but he was solid.

Then there was Luis Gonzalez. It is to belabor the point that no rational, i.e., *natural* explanation answers the question, *how did he hit 57 home runs?* He just did, leave it at that. He batted .325, driving in an unreal 142 runs. If Bell, Williams, and Finley did not have career years, Gonzo made up for them by having one for the new millennium.

Finley hit .275, playing impeccable defense. Reggie Sanders came on as a free agent. The born-again Christian from Florence, South Carolina, fit right into the Colangelo scheme. A good player in Cincinnati with pop, he exceeded expectations by slamming 33 home runs with 90 RBIs. Damian Miller was as solid as a rock behind the dish, in many ways the central casting version of what Hollywood would call "a big-league catcher."

Utilityman Craig Counsell was excellent when called on and would play a big role in postseason play. Danny Bautista, Dave Dellucci, Rod Barajas, and Erubiel Durazo also contributed.

On the mound of course there was the Big Unit, earning big money with a Cy Young season of 21–6 with a 2.49 ERA, which was more dominant than even those numbers reveal.

Then there was Schilling. His 22–6 record, to go with a 2.98 ERA, was every bit as dominant as Johnson's. These are herein just words in a book, but some historical analysis is called for. He was *just as dominant as Johnson*, and Johnson in 2001 was in the middle of a stretch in which he was as dominant as any pitcher who ever lived. This includes Sandy Koufax and Tom Seaver, modern heroes of the Unit. The statistics of "dark age" hurlers such as Christy Mathewson and Walter Johnson are more gaudy, but their multiple 30-win seasons, translated into the 2000s, look like what Johnson and Schilling were doing at a time in which the parks were smaller, everybody said the ball was livelier, the hitters lived in weight rooms, and now we know they were enhanced by steroids. Of course, now we also know pitchers were not so innocent when it comes to drug usage, but this is a tiresome point for another book, so we will keep the talk to baseball. As good as Schilling was in the regular season, it was really just a prelude for later heroics.

After the "Spahn and Sain and pray for rain" combo of Johnson and Schilling, there was not much else. There was Miguel Batista, Brian Anderson, Robert Ellis, Albie Lopez, Greg Swindell, Troy Brohawn, Bret Prinz, and Erik Sabel. To quote Gertrude Stein's description of Oakland, California, there was "no there there."

The closer: Byung-Hyun Kim. He looked like the "next big thing" when he first broke in, but that effect had lasted for a few exhibition games and an early season go-around, not much else. That said, he could be effective, and was fairly so in 2001. Nobody was mistaking him for Dennis Eckersley, but those guys are few and far between.

Dodger Stadium opened the first act, with Johnson imitating Koufax in besting L.A. 3–2. Schilling looked like Don Drysdale, 7–2, in front of fans who lamented that the new "Koufax-Drysdale Show" was now a road act playing in a desert town not so near to them anymore.

By June, Arizona was 32–22. Schilling improved to 9–1 with a 4–2 victory over San Diego. Johnson was good but not quite at full throttle. Baseball, however, was not looking much at Arizona. Two thousand one was a super year. In Seattle, Japanese import Ichiro Suzuki was off the charts good, as was his team. Bret Boone, a journeyman, now looked more like Rogers Hornsby. Oh, the belabored question of steroids?

Oakland, led by another one of *those* guys, Jason Giambi, started slow but was picking up ground. The Yankees were baseball's version of the American Army, liberating towns and villages in an unprecedented display of force.

But the real story was Bonds, Barry Bonds. In May he put on a display in Atlanta for the ages. It seemed like Big Mac's record would fall like Poland during the *blitzkrieg* by the same date as that event: September 1.

Bob Brenly and pitching guru Roger Craig discuss plans for pitchers and catchers in the first workouts of the 2001 season in Tucson.

The D'backs just kept on plugging away throughout the summer, which developed into a race for first place with San Francisco and Los Angeles. The wild card was the second prize, with Houston and St. Louis making bids from the Central Division.

On August 28 Johnson won his 18th game, 4–1 over the Giants at Chase. Interest in the race, and in Bonds' full pursuit of McGwire, was at a fever pitch. The Johnson-Bonds match-up was Bob Feller–Joe DiMaggio stuff, with the Unit prevailing this time. His team held onto first place at 76–55.

A week later, Schilling beat the Giants in San Francisco 7–2. The adage that "good pitching beats good hitting" favored Arizona. They continued to hold off Bonds and company to stay in first place (79–60).

On Sunday, September 9, the club trounced San Diego. Baseball interest was enormous, with tight races between new champions and traditional franchises and with great cities like New York and St. Louis drawing big crowds. Records were being sought. Bonds was going for his 70. Seattle eyed the Yankees AL mark of 114 wins from 1998, and the Cubs all-time 116 victories of 1906.

On Tuesday, September 11, 2001, the world stood still.

Baseball resumed on September 17, and a funny thing happened. Nobody cared...for a few days. But after a game or three, it became a beautiful diversion. The D'backs took two of three from Los Angeles, holding off San Francisco. They were through playing against Bonds, who of course did break the record, but in a losing cause. Arizona clinched it the final Saturday.

Victory Starts at Home

Arizona entered the 2001 playoffs with the decided advantage of Randy Johnson and Curt Schilling. The postseason is much different from the regular season, when a manager must use his bench, make use of depth, rely on third, fourth, and fifth starters, and a deep bullpen.

A couple of great starters—and preferably one great closer—can get it done in a short-series format. Of course, since the 1993 expansion, baseball had adopted an extra series. The more games played, the more depth would make a difference.

That said, entering the 2001 postseason, the Johnson-Schilling combination was not quite the Koufax-Drysdale model it was later compared to. They had of course both dominated during the regular season in Koufax-Drysdale form, but the Dodgers duo made its name on the strength of World Series pitching.

Schilling had pitched brilliantly for Philadelphia in the 1993 postseason, but that was his only appearance and it was eight years in the past. Johnson was *winless* in playoff games since 1995. His crusade was one of atonement.

The Division Series matched Arizona with St. Louis. Tony LaRussa's club was always tough. Slugger Mark McGwire, beset by the kind of nagging injuries caused by steroids, was virtually a non-factor, but rookie Albert Pujols emerged as the next great star of the game.

Schilling got the opening nod at Chase Field against 22-game winner Matt Morris. He threw a complete game—a three-hit, 1–0 shutout—setting the tone for the club's October strategy. It was just the ninth shutout and fifth complete game of the format. Steve Finley's two-out single in the fifth scored Damian Miller. That was the game.

Johnson continued his October struggles when Pujols hit a two-run homer off of him in the first inning, spurring St. Louis to a 4–1 win. At Busch Stadium, Counsell's three-run homer in the seventh off of Mike Matthews lifted Arizona to a key 5–3 win. St. Louis had to touch Arizona's second-tier starters if they had a chance, and they did that by knocking Albie Lopez around in the fourth game.

Schilling pitched the fifth game at home. Reggie Sanders hit a home run. J. D. Drew's homer tied it 1–1 in the eighth. It was the first run Schilling had given up in postseason play over 25 innings, a record approaching the marks of Babe Ruth and Whitey Ford. In the bottom of the ninth, Tony Womack's two-out RBI single sent the Cardinals home...again. LaRussa's clubs in Oakland and now in St. Louis consistently had great talent that underperformed in October.

In the Championship Series, Johnson had a monkey on his back in the form of a seven-game playoff losing streak. He faced the legendary Greg Maddux at Chase. It was a classic match won by the Big Unit 2–0. He struck out 11 hitters.

Atlanta won the second game 8–1 over Miguel Batista, who retired 13 straight at one point but could not hold the fort. The series shifted to Turner Field, where Arizona had won all three games in 2001. Schilling struck out 12 in a solid 5–1 win. Finley drove in three runs. Counsell was 3-for-4.

Maddux was the victim of bad defense in the fourth game, falling 11–4 in the fourth game. Johnson wrapped it up in Atlanta 3–2. Johnson pitched seven innings, striking out Brian Jordan with the bases loaded in the seventh. Byung-Hyun Kim's scoreless eighth and ninth earned him the save. Erubiel Durazo's two-run homer off Tom Glavine was the winning margin. Craig Counsell's .381 average earned him series MVP honors.

Next: the Yankees. Joe Torre's crew was at the height of their powers, but this time around they had the rare advantage of being

DID YOU KNOW . . . That while the Yankees entered the series having won three straight World Championships, Miguel Batista had won the seventh and final game of the 2001 Caribbean World Series on February 7?

Not since the days of Koufax and Drysdale did a lefty and a righty on the same staff dominate opponents the way Randy Johnson and Curt Schilling did for the Diamondbacks. In 2001 they were Ace No. 1 and Ace No. 2, two 20-game winners and Cy Young frontrunners.

sentimental favorites. Rooting for the Yankees, as it was said long ago, is like "rooting for U.S. Steel." A popular Broadway play in the 1950s, *Damn Yankees,* was based on the notion that the only way to beat them was to make a deal with the devil.

The Bronx Bombers looked like "Black Jack" Pershing's forces knocking the Germans out of the Argonne, Sherman on the march to Atlanta, in winning four of the previous five World Series in a manner every bit as impressive as their 1920s, 1930s, 1940s, 1950s, 1960s, and 1970s counterparts.

All but die-hard Yankees fans rooted for anybody to win except the Yankees. But 9/11 changed all that. At first, baseball seemed utterly

TRIVIA

How many world championships did the Yankees have entering the 2001 World Series?

Answers to the trivia questions are on pages 159–160.

unimportant, but when the games resumed, it provided to be a balm of Gilead for the American psyche.

In 1942 Commissioner Kenesaw Mountain Landis approached President Franklin Roosevelt, suggesting that baseball suspend operations in order to mobilize for the war effort. FDR, a perceptive judge of public emotion, declined in favor of the morale boosting effect of the national pastime. In retrospect, the fact that America could turn back Hitler and Tojo—a two-front war on three continents, myriad islands, waterways, and skies, all fought in entrenched enemy territory—while playing sports at home is an accomplishment over and above that of any previous empire, power, or nation-state. The U.S.S.R., by contrast, expended every last bit of its treasure, natural resources, manpower, and energy in holding off one army on their home turf in what amounted to a war of attrition.

When baseball came back, Barry Bonds's unbelievable pursuit of Mark McGwire's home-run record captivated the nation. Then the Yankees beat Oakland in an unreal Divisional Series. The wild-card A's went into Yankee Stadium. New Yorkers seemed to be putting up a brave front while Oakland swept two straight. Not this year, it seemed. With everything that had happened, nobody could expect the Yanks to have their hearts in it.

The series shifted to Oakland. Derek Jeter made a backhanded relay toss that goes down in history with "the Catch" by Willie Mays in the 1954 World Series. It saved a 1–0 win. New York came back. In Game 5 at Yankee Stadium, the crowd went wild. If terrorists thought they had broken our spirit, they discovered to their horror they had simply united the greatest people on the face of the Earth. The A's sensed that now they were merely players on a Shakespearean stage, with a final act written not for them. They were right. New York took a city and a country on their backs.

The 116-win Mariners were next, but they were no match for the steamrolling pinstripers, who sent them home in five games.

Arizona was a fine club, but they were just bit players in this drama, it appeared. A fourth-year expansion team with funny uniforms, playing in a nice Southwestern town in a new stadium with no history. Along came the Bronx Bombers, dripping with tradition and polish; now riding the sentiment of a great sports story, apparently being written by the Hand of Destiny.

How the War on Terror Was Won

It was October 27 when the Series opened at Chase Field. The events of September 11 had pushed the whole season back, but of course weather was no concern in the desert. Schilling faced the creditable Mike Mussina. Luis Gonzalez's two-run homer ignited a four-run fourth. They added four more to put it away. Schilling went seven, was untouchable as usual, and Arizona had a 9–1 win.

Randy Johnson fanned 11 and tossed a three-hit shutout on Sunday night. Matt Williams's three-run homer in the seventh padded the Unit's 4–0 win. Matt's homer made him the first player in history to hit World Series homers for three different teams: Giants, Indians, and D'backs.

The Diamondbacks were confident as they congratulated themselves on the Chase turf, but when they arrived in the Big Apple all bets were off. The atmosphere was electric. New York's comeback against Oakland had ignited the sense of destiny that hung palpably in the air. Arizona would have to go to their second-tier starters.

The town was riding a Yankees wave—equal parts baseball fever and reaction to the September 11 tragedy. When Arizona got to the Stadium on Tuesday, it was like entering the Roman Coliseum. The crowds never let up from the time they arrived. Mayor Rudy Giuliani was there. President Bush was there. The threat was enormous— another plane, a bomb, a hand-held missile, chemicals, Anthrax, God knows what. New Yorkers just *thumbed their nose* at the terrorists, daring them to try something again. It was as if they were repelling evil by the sheer goodness of their *American nature*!

For the Diamondbacks, the whole crazy scene—the standing ovation for two Republicans in a Democrat town, a sense of wild celebration—was intoxicating. What was their role here? It was exciting and they were patriots, too—happy to see New York back on its feet so soon—but they had a job to do. The 2–0 lead that looked so great in Arizona looked like a flat-footed tie at Yankee Stadium.

The performance of "Rocket" Roger Clemens provided no boost to their confidence when he beat Brian Anderson 2–1. It was a tough "waste" of a great performance by one of their "other" pitchers. Mariano Rivera struck out four of six Arizona hitters—looking as dominant as a pitcher can look—to close it out. The crowd went berserk.

Schilling talked Bob Brenly into letting him pitch Game 4. The momentum was so strong in the Yankees' favor under these conditions that Schilling knew it would take a heroic performance only he was capable of to stem the tide. He gave up a solo homer to Shane Spencer, but only three hits in seven innings on three days' rest. Mark Grace homered off Orlando Hernandez. In the top of the eighth, on Halloween night, the D'backs scored twice to lead 3–1, but there were still tricks and treats in store.

Enter Byung-Hyun Kim. Every fan in Yankee Stadium knew instinctively what would happen next: they would light the Korean import up like a Christmas tree. When Kim set New York down with three strikeouts, Arizona players looked at each other as if to say, *Is this gonna happen?*

It happened, all right, but not the way they wanted it to. Forces of nature swirled about Yankee Stadium like so much stardust. New York did not just hit three homers to knock the thing off; they had too much sense of drama for that. They waited until there were two outs and a man on to spring their trap. Tino Martinez got hold of Kim's first pitch, hitting it over the center-field fence: 3–3.

Mariano Rivera set the D'backs down like pony leaguers. They had as much chance as a one-legged man in a butt-kickin' contest. The clock struck midnight. The Witching Hour. Kim, desperate to

That the tradition of playing the National Anthem began as a patriotic gesture during World War II?

Luis Gonzalez celebrates driving in the winning run in the ninth inning of Game 7 of the 2001 World Series against the Yankees.

atone for his ninth-inning sin, set two Yanks down, then went to a full count on Derek Jeter. Kim looked like a deer caught in the headlights when Derek announced to the populace, "I have arrived as a New York sports icon" by homering down the right-field line to give his team the 4–3 victory. The atmosphere was as fantastic as has ever been in an American sports stadium.

Miguel Batista was told to stem the momentum in Game 5. He did it with 7⅔ strong innings. Finley and Rod Barajas hit homers. Arizona led 2–0 into the ninth. Hello Mr. Kim.

"If you can make it here, you can make it anywhere," the old song says, but inherent in those lyrics is the fact that it's a lot easier said than done. The sound just *emanated* from the big crowd as the curtain rose in the bottom of the ninth. When Jorge Posada doubled to lead off, the script was almost too obvious, but there were still some plot twists.

Scott Brosius, a nice player who has never been mistaken with Reggie Jackson, got hold of a Kim riser, depositing it into the stands for a game-tying homer. The camera panned in on poor Kim, the loneliest man in the world.

Of course, the Yanks would win, but only after applying maximum heartbreak to the Arizona upstarts. The tenth inning: scoreless. The eleventh: Arizona put runners on first and second, then advanced them to second and third with a sacrifice bunt. It was a bit of "little ball" that Brenly was criticized about. Giving up an out against Rivera was like donating money to the IRS.

Finley was walked intentionally. Reggie Sanders hit a shot up the middle, but Alfonso Soriano's diving catch was almost too much for the Yankees faithful to take. They still had more in store. Mark Grace bounced into an inning-ending out, and the place was spasmodic— the beams of the old structure lifted off the ground by the strength of emotion. This was the most exciting World Series ever played in Yankee Stadium, which is one heckuva statement.

The announcers almost lost their ability to describe the action, so riveting was it. The sense of doom in the D'backs dugout could not be pushed back. What next? So the Yankees came up and won it, right? Wrong. They were held. On to the twelfth, well into the early morning hours in the dark of the Autumn Bronx night. Arizona was set down.

TRIVIA

What baseball tradition started after 9/11 that is still adhered to?

Answers to the trivia questions are on pages 159–160.

In the bottom of the inning, facing Albie Lopez, Chuck Knoblauch singled. Brosius bunted him over. Soriano (naturally) came up and singled. Knoblauch raced home. Yankee Stadium…well, you know what happened. Words do not do the scene justice.

"This is the most incredible couple of games I've ever managed," said Joe Torre. No team had ever won two World Series games when trailing by two or more runs going into the ninth inning.

The Price of Victory

At some point during the flight back to Phoenix, Arizona, the D'backs—who might have needed a few cocktails to assuage the sensory overload of the whole New York experience—started to curl their lips into the smallest of little smiles at the whole absurd week that still was.

First, there was the realization that win, lose, or draw, they were part of something very special. Every baseball player starting in Little League dreams of playing in the World Series, and here they were.

Next, they knew that despite all the Yankee Stadium craziness they were still alive—very much alive—Arizona had home-field edge with Johnson and Schilling tanned, rested, and ready to go.

"The attitude on this club was, 'Geez, you know, we can't believe this happened again!'" Williams recalled. "But going back on the plane, we talked about it. We talked about the fact that we've got Randy and Curt going the next two games and we had that playoff experience of how dominating they were in the two previous series. So we took solace in that and we thought, 'Well, you know, we've got a shot here. We need to win the first game and then we've got a real chance here.'"

"When the playoffs started, a lot of people said and wrote, 'Well, you can't win with just two pitchers,' to which I would always respond, 'It depends which two,'" said Joe Garagiola Jr.

A curious crowd came to Chase Field for Game 6. It was as if this were

TRIVIA

What was the combined record of Randy Johnson and Curt Schilling in the 2001 fall classic?

Answers to the trivia questions are on pages 159–160.

97

an entirely different Series; two new teams in another season than the one played a week earlier.

The whole 9/11 experience had been brought to them, too. Naturally, Arizonans grieved and agonized over the events, as had all Americans. But the past week had demonstrated how much of an East Coast thing it had been—a New York event that shook the world, yes, but in the Valley of the Sun, surrounded by desert, there was a sense that it did not reach this far. When the New York Yankees appeared on their field, they brought the whole thing into their house.

Then there was the second-guessing of Bob Brenly, who was getting the big bucks to leave no stone unturned in thinking of everything in order to give his club a chance to win. He was inexperienced and it showed. His decision to squeeze with a left-handed batter against a southpaw who lives on off-the-corner sliders in the World Series was brutal, but he got away with it. He did not get away with his omission in New York.

How come Brenly never used ace lefty Randy Johnson in relief at the end of either Games 4 or 5 at Yankee Stadium? Johnson pitched a complete game shutout on Sunday in Phoenix, and at that point it was decided he would not start again until Saturday night at Chase Field. He normally pitched on four days' rest, but in this case the Big Unit had five days to sit his butt in planes, buses, autos, hotel rooms, and on dugout benches. He likely did some long toss and light bullpen work on Tuesday, followed by some more bullpen work on Thursday. Or, if he normally only goes once on the side between starts, Wednesday would have been that day.

Brenly and pitching coach Bob Welch should have decided on Sunday that Johnson not throw on the side on Tuesday. Instead of having him throw before the game Wednesday, he should have been sent to the bullpen to get ready late in Schilling's game. Byung-Hyun Kim was not a good bet to get six outs. Johnson should have come in for the last one or two outs on Wednesday, instead of Kim sticking around long enough to hang a rising slider to Tino Martinez and later flatten one into Derek Jeter's zone. The relief appearance would have amounted to Johnson's sideline work, whether he was brought in or not. If Johnson did not throw on the side before Wednesday's game or in the late innings, he should not have thrown at all.

Pitchers Randy Johnson and Mike Morgan celebrate the Diamondbacks' 3–2 victory over the Yankees in Game 7 of the World Series.

If he warmed up Wednesday only, or warmed up and pitched, that should have been his only between-starts work, and he would not have been used Thursday. He only should have thrown Wednesday as part of late-game strategy.

On Thursday, he should have been fresh, not having thrown at all since his last start, and again should have been ready by not throwing before the game. Brenly should have used him in the ninth to get the last one to two outs, no more. If Johnson was not used and

By the
NUMBERS .183—The Yankees' batting average versus
Arizona pitching in the 2001 World Series; their lowest
since a four-game sweep at the hands of the Dodgers' Sandy
Koufax and Don Drysdale in 1963.

did not warm up, he then could have gone to the pen with a catcher after midnight to get the 15 minutes of work that he had been held out of over the previous couple days.

Yes, the whole effort would not have been his regular routine, but he had an extra day of rest anyway. The World Series is not supposed to be routine. It's possible that Brenly and Welch went to the Unit, and Randy told them he could not be ready on Saturday if this scenario were to take place. The guess here is nobody thought about it. It takes a little planning and some calculation, but it was not all that complicated.

With all of this national psychoanalysis, something really curious happened. The Yanks rolled over and died. Johnson dominated them, but *again* Brenly screwed up. Whereas before he should have *used* Johnson, now he should *not* have used him.

In the third inning Arizona scored eight runs to lead 12–0. Brenly should have taken Johnson out of the game right then, sent him to the trainer for icing, and told him to be ready to throw in relief on Sunday. The game was over, and winning the World Series was more important than Johnson getting credit for the victory, which he needed to pitch five complete innings in order to attain.

Brenly should have used the lowest end of his bullpen, saving all his best arms for use on Sunday, if needed. Instead, he stayed with Johnson for seven, effectively making him unusable on Sunday. Arizona rolled to a 15–2 win.

Victory

It was inevitable that such a Series would go seven. In that seventh game it was Schilling versus Clemens in a duel for the ages. It was November 4, but baseball fever gripped the nation. Clemens and Schilling matched goose eggs until the sixth, when Danny Bautista doubled home a run to give the home team a 1–0 edge. Could Schilling go the distance? It seemed that he would have to. Experience had taught that hard lesson.

In the top of the seventh, however, Tino Martinez's RBI single tied it up. Schilling, pitching on three day's rest for the second straight game, was visually tiring. In the eighth his split-fingered fastball hung just enough for Soriano to golf it into the stands for a 2–1 Yankees lead. After 7⅓ innings, Schilling left the mound with a man on base.

The camera caught his face. He had a disbelieving expression, like Superman getting the first dose of Kryptonite. This was Arizona's rock, their last line of defense. If Schilling could be beaten, what hope was there? The Yankees' destiny was to win not just for New York, but for the American people, right?

Miguel Batista came on to get the second out. Then Johnson was brought in. It was risky. Had he pitched only four or five innings on Saturday, he might have been expected to have more gas in the tank. But he had adrenaline and it was enough. Johnson got the last out in the eighth and pitched a scoreless top of the ninth.

"That to me is an element of that game that has been so overlooked it's staggering," Garagiola remarked of the fact Johnson had never been a relief pitcher.

"Relieving in the seventh game of the World Series wasn't that big a deal to me," Johnson modestly said. "I was trying to go out and

The Diamondbacks gather for a group hug after beating the Yankees in the World Series.

do whatever it took. When a World Series is in your grasp like that, it's not too hard to get up for it."

Brenly was not off the hook in that his use of Johnson on Saturday restricted him to an inning or two at most on Sunday. Had he rested him, and had the seventh game gone into extra innings, the Big Unit might have had four or five innings in him. It was all moot unless Arizona could score off the untouchable Mariano Rivera.

"We had come off the field into the dugout, and Gracie was screaming the old Tug McGraw line, 'Ya gotta believe! Ya gotta believe!'" said Brenly. "I looked down the bench and there was not one guy with his head down. Everybody was positive."

"I'm a little too young to have seen McGraw pitch, so he never came to my mind," Grace said, but he admitted that he was yellin' and screamin'. "We had two cracks at Rivera. It looked kind of bleak. You can say, 'We're gonna get him,' but realistically we were in trouble."

Grace led off against the "lights out" relief ace, arguably the greatest in the game's history, and in 2001 at the apex of his abilities. Furthermore, Grace carried a .133 Series average to the plate against him, but he had two hits in this one.

"Amazing Gracie" stroked a single to center field. It had started to rain earlier in the game, a rare thing in Phoenix. With the roof open under warm skies, the moisture was felt. David Dellucci decided it was a good omen, that "something in the air felt good."

Damian Miller carried three strikeouts in this game to the plate. He was asked to sacrifice Dellucci, pinch-running for Grace, to second. His bunt was back to the pitcher, who threw it into center field, trying for Dellucci. Midre Cummings came in to run for Dellucci. Jay Bell pinch-hit for Johnson. Brenly was now off the hook in terms of his "overuse" of Randy the previous day.

Bell bunted, but Rivera, who despite his error was an excellent fielder, responded this time with a cat-quick throw to third, getting Dellucci. Now there was one out with runners at first and second. Womack came to the plate.

"This is what you dream of as a little kid: bottom of the ninth, the World Series," recalled Womack.

The count went to 2–0. Womack got a pitch to hit but fouled it off. If he hit a ground ball on the fast Chase Field turf, he would have to use every ounce of his speed to avoid a season-ending double play. Rivera basically had one pitch, a cut fastball. Knowing it is coming does not make it hittable, but Womack guessed location—in—and was right. It was a 95 mph cutter instead of the 97 mph outside fastball. Normally, the inside cutter saws bats in half, but Womack was looking in and smacked a double. The score was tied. Womack looked to the sky above the open Chase roof. His father had recently passed away.

Counsell, 0-for-19, stepped to the plate with men on second and third. He was hit by a pitch to load them up. Torre decided to move

DID YOU KNOW . . . That entering Game 7 of the 2001 World Series, the D'backs had outscored New York 28–3 in their three wins. The Yankees had outscored Arizona 9–6 in their three victories.

his infield in instead of playing for a double play. Luis Gonzalez stepped to the plate.

"In any kid's dream, the ideal situation would be to hit a home run, but in real life for me it was more important to make contact, get the ball in play, and make something happen," he said.

With the count at one strike, Gonzo got a cutter on the hands. He flared one out toward left-center. Had Jeter been playing for two, he might have had a chance, but he was on the grass and that was it. Bell scored, and Arizona was the world champion.

For just a brief second there was a sense that the script had been altered, that after the World Trade Center went down New York deserved this. But that realization was replaced by a moment of greater clarity. New York had gotten their life back courtesy of its national game, win or lose. When Arizona won the World Series, it was a way of saying that all of America, not just one city, had won. It had been fought cleanly, bravely, by two great teams who both deserved it. It was an honor to be a part of it, no matter the victor.

"You have to tip your cap to the Yankees," said Gonzo, a man of great class. "As much adversity as they had gone through and all the tragedies that had happened in New York on September 11 made for a great drama on TV."

TOP 10

Greatest Seventh Games in World Series History

(Diamondbacks in bold)
1. **2001 D'backs-Yankees**
2. 1960 Pirates-Yankees
3. 1997 Marlins-Indians
4. 1946 Cardinals-Red Sox
5. 1962 Yankees-Giants
6. 1924 Senators-Giants
7. 1972 A's-Reds
8. 1955 Dodgers-Yankees
9. 1975 Reds-Red Sox
10. 1926 Cardinals-Yankees

The Lucky Manager

Bob Brenly did a good job managing the Arizona Diamondbacks. He is a fine baseball man who has been around the game a long time. But he was lucky to win the 2001 World Series. First, he had a team with fantastic talent, especially at the most important position on the field: starting pitcher.

He is also lucky that some questionable strategic moves did not cost his team the title. He should have used Johnson in relief in one or two of the blown-save games in New York. He also should have held Johnson out when the club went way up in Game 6, so he could reserve him for more than an inning and a third of seventh-game relief. As it was, Johnson gave him that inning and a third. The Unit was removed for a pinch-hitter, which was a move that had to be made. However, if Johnson's turn at bat had not come up, and Arizona only tied the score, Johnson might have been needed for four extra innings or so. Having pitched four extra Saturday innings after going up by an insurmountable 12–0 score, he probably would not have been able to handle it. Brenly was lucky he was not left to face that circumstance.

That said, Brenly deserved credit for winning with a shaky starting rotation after his first two guns, and for prevailing despite Byung-Hyun Kim. His middle relief did pretty well.

Brenly was born in 1954 in Ohio, then attended Ohio University. A 6′2″, 210-pound catcher, he signed with San Francisco, playing under some good managers there. This included Frank Robinson, a hard-nosed type, and Roger Craig, known for his handling of pitchers. Craig was one of the biggest promoters of the split-fingered fastball, which helped revolutionize pitching. Chicago's Bruce Sutter

rose to stardom with it, and Craig taught it to everybody. Brenly was the catcher who handled those pitchers.

Brenly played nine seasons in the major leagues. He made the most of limited ability. He could be compared to Mike Scioscia, another catcher from neighboring Pennsylvania who played for the Dodgers in contemporary times before becoming a successful manager. Brenly hit .247. He was a journeyman. He played on San Francisco's 1987 division champions, but was released before the 1989 World Series year. Brenly represented Craig's "Hum Baby" attitude—upbeat and enthusiastic.

Brenly's first year as a big-league manager was in 2001. He replaced Buck Showalter. The theory was that Showalter's "tight ship" methods were needed to build a young franchise. By 2001 they were a veteran team filled with rich free agents. Brenly was considered the more appropriate man to handle "grown-ups." Showalter took the club to 100 wins in 1999 but slumped in 2000. The division was very competitive. Brenly's hire certainly was a good one, lucky or not. Colangelo's insistence on a certain "type" of player (read: anti–Barry Bonds) seemed to provide the club with good karma. Luck broke their way. Read into that whatever you want to.

The 2001 Diamondbacks were 92–70, but the 2002 club was even better at 98–64. Sitting in the favorite's role, with Johnson and Schilling even more dominant than in 2001, Brenly's club did not make it through the postseason this time. San Francisco and Anaheim survived the wild-card road, with the Angels taking the brass ring.

After that, Brenly's team plummeted to 84–78 and then 29–50 before his 2004 firing. They got old fast. Stars departed via free agency. They did not survive the transitional period that marks good teams from dynasties. Brenly's managerial record in Arizona: 303–262 (.536).

Brenly started as a third baseman, and at Ohio University he tied Mike Schmidt's single-season home-run record. He switched to

Bob Brenly, joined by son Michael, watches his team work out at Chase Field prior to Game 1 of the 2001 National League Championship Series against the Atlanta Braves.

catcher in 1979, his fourth pro season. He continued to fill in at third or first base when necessary in the majors, playing 45 games at third in 1986.

In the fourth game of the 1987 championship series he homered off the Cardinals' Danny Cox. In the fourth inning of a game against the Braves on September 14, 1986, Brenly tied a major league record with four errors at third base, booting three grounders and throwing wildly once to allow four unearned runs. In the fifth inning he hit a solo home run. In the seventh he added a two-run single to tie the score 6–6. In the bottom of the ninth, with two out and the count full, he homered to win the game.

Brenly was hitting only .189 when the Giants released him in 1988. The Blue Jays signed him but released him, so he was not part of the club that lost to Oakland in the 1989 playoffs.

Brenly achieved great popularity in San Francisco. After his retirement, he became a Giants coach. After several seasons in the broadcast booth, Brenly was hired to replace Showalter.

Brenly may be like former UCLA basketball coach Steve Lavin, in that while he enjoyed success as a manager, his friendly personality might be more suited for the broadcasting booth. In 2005 the Chicago Cubs hired him as their color analyst on the wide-ranging WGN radio station.

Brenly previously worked in the Cubs booth during the 1990–1991 seasons. After being let go by Arizona, he joined the Fox broadcast team for the second time, as an analyst during the 2004 National League Championship Series.

Brenly began his television broadcast career in 1996, working for FOX during marquee baseball events, including the All-Star Game, NLCS, and the World Series. After a two-year stint with FOX, Brenly spent three seasons as a member of the Arizona Diamondbacks broadcast team before moving into the dugout.

Brenly also coached for three years on Dusty Baker's staff in San Francisco. He made the 1984 All-Star Game. He and his wife, Joan, have a daughter, Lacey, and a son, Michael. They lived in Scottsdale during his Diamondbacks years. Brenly earned a bachelor of science degree in health education from Ohio U. He was inducted into the school's Hall of Fame in 1988.

His media experience is greater than his managerial experience. He hosted *The Bob Brenly Show* after Giants games in 1988 on KNBR. This became a tradition many players in San Francisco have followed. Even Jeff Kent gave of his time to be on a weekly show when he was there. The show is credited with helping create the team's popularity, which went from low attendance and almost leaving for

TOP 10

Greatest Pitching Combos

(Diamondbacks in bold)

1. Sandy Koufax–Don Drysdale
2. Christy Mathewson–Joe McGinnity
3. Bob Feller–Bob Lemon
4. Waite Hoyt–Herb Pennock
5. Chief Bender–Eddie Plank
6. Greg Maddux–John Smoltz
7. Christy Mathewson–Rube Marquard
8. Catfish Hunter–Vida Blue
9. Juan Marichal–Gaylord Perry
10. Randy Johnson–Curt Schilling

Tampa in 1992–1993, to the building of a new, sold-out stadium in the 2000s.

Brenly has been quoted as saying the my-way-or-the-highway approach of so many managers and coaches "just doesn't work anymore." Brenly did not go so far as to say the Johnson-Schilling duo he managed was better than Sandy Koufax and Don Drysdale, but he said perhaps only the Dodgers combo was better, at least in the sense of the righty-lefty dynamic.

When Brenly left Baker's coaching staff, it looked as if he was leaving his chance at a managing career behind, but opportunities just presented themselves. He seemed to be in the right place at the right time—time after time. He has continually been lucky, but as Branch Rickey said, "Luck is the residue of design."

The Big Unit

The 1984 Trojans might have been the most under-performing college baseball team of all time since they had the sophomore Randy Johnson and junior first baseman Mark McGwire. Big Mac, an All-American in 1983, led the nation with 32 homers and earned National Player of the Year honors in 1984. Instead of earning Dedeaux his 12th College World Series title, however, they were beaten in the Fresno regionals.

Johnson was decidedly unspectacular, going 5–3 with a 3.35 ERA, striking out 73 hitters in 78 innings. He, McGwire, and teammate Sid Akins were chosen to play for the 1984 U.S. Olympic team. In retrospect, this team is thought to be the finest amateur team ever assembled, and another under-performing one, too. Mississippi State's Will Clark, Rafael Palmeiro, and Bobby Thigpen were just a few of the future major league stars who played for the team, coached by Dedeaux. Like Dedeaux's Trojans, though, they failed in the end, losing to Japan at Dodger Stadium, settling for Silver at the L.A. Games.

As a junior, Johnson seemed to regress, going 6–9 with a 5.32 ERA. He was like Mark Langston, a southpaw at San Jose State who was drafted high and accorded great promise on the strength of potential, despite a poor record his junior year.

Unlike McGwire, a first-round pick by Oakland who was fast-tracked to the big leagues, Johnson was drafted after a few rounds by Montreal. He was tagged a "project" and was by no means a "can't miss" minor league prospect. He came up to the major leagues with Montreal in 1988, struggling for three seasons, and was traded to Seattle along the way.

In 1990, the year he turned 27, the 6'10" Johnson turned the corner, winning 14 games for the Mariners. His progress was similar to that of Sandy Koufax. Finally in 1993, the year of his 30th birthday, Johnson became truly dominant. He won 19 games and struck out a mind-boggling 308 batters in 255⅓ innings.

In the 1990s Johnson and his USC teammate McGwire became the two most intimidating players in the game—players of great size and godlike power. Randy developed into one of the fastest pitchers of all time, a strikeout artist to rank alongside the all-time best: Nolan Ryan, Steve Carlton, Tom Seaver, Bob Feller, Walter Johnson, Lefty Grove, Sandy Koufax, and Roger Clemens.

Johnson sought out power pitchers for advice. When his team played the Yankees, Johnson found New York announcer Tom Seaver. But it was Nolan Ryan who took him under his wing, giving him words of wisdom which he learned to live by.

Off the field, Johnson was just what Jerry Colangelo wanted: a family man of sensitive persuasions who is an avid photographer.

In 1995 Johnson demonstrated that he was bidding for all-time greatness, winning 18 against two defeats with a 2.48 ERA and 294 strikeouts in 214⅓ innings. He pitched Seattle to a stirring stretch-run division title, defeating Langston on the season's last day to win it. It earned him his first Cy Young Award.

He narrowly missed becoming the first AL triple crown pitcher—leading the league in wins, ERA, and strikeouts—since Detroit's Hal Newhouser accomplished the feat in 1945. His .900 winning percentage broke Ron Guidry's 1978 record. His strikeouts-per-nine-innings ratio of 12.35 broke the record held by Ryan.

In the 1995 AL Division Series, Johnson came through again with a brilliant playoff performance against the Yankees in Game 3,

DID YOU KNOW . . . That Randy Johnson has won five Cy Young Awards (one in the American League)? Roger Clemens has seven. Tom Seaver, Sandy Koufax, and Jim Palmer won three. His alma mater, the University of Southern California, boasts nine Cy Youngs, since Seaver and Barry Zito are Trojans, too.

holding the Bronx Bombers to two runs in seven innings, helping the Mariners avoid a three-game sweep.

After Seattle won Game 4 by the score of 11–8 in the Kingdome, Johnson came out of the bullpen with one day of rest. Despite allowing the go-ahead run to New York in the eleventh inning, Johnson received credit for the victory after the Mariners staged a stirring victory in their final at-bat.

Entering the 1998 season, Johnson's career ratio of 10.38 Ks per nine innings pitched was the best ever, topping Ryan's 9.59. In 1997 he set an American League record for left-handers by striking out 19 batters in a 4–1 loss to the Oakland A's. On August 8 he matched the feat by setting down 19 White Sox. Posting a 20–4 record (including 16 straight going back to 1995) with 291 strikeouts and an ERA of 2.28, Johnson finished second in the Cy Young balloting to Toronto's Roger Clemens.

Not unlike the reaction to "Sudden" Sam McDowell in the 1960s, Johnson had the effect of starting "colds," "flus," and various other maladies sidelining some of the best left-handed sticks in the game.

Johnson threw as hard as anybody, partly from the side. At his height and reach, he was scarier than any pitcher ever has been. He demonstrated a willingness to work inside, just as Bob Gibson and Seaver did. His slider was almost as wicked as Carlton's in his prime. In the 1993 All-Star Game, Johnson brushed Philadelphia's John Kruk off the plate with a ball that landed halfway up the backstop screen. Kruk struck out without trying, halfway joking, but not entirely. Colorado's Larry Walker, in an All-Star appearance four years later, turned his batting helmet around and switched to the other side of the plate. Johnson just laughed.

Johnson led the majors in hit batsmen for two consecutive seasons. Cleveland's Kenny Lofton claimed Johnson had been throwing at him for years. Johnson, who never hit Lofton in his career, said, "I could hit someone across the other dugout if I wanted to. And I can surely hit someone 60′6″ inches away, someone 6′ tall and 185 pounds and not moving."

In 1998 Johnson was thinking about playing in Arizona, where he bought a home in a fashionable neighborhood. He vowed to some day play for the D'backs, but Randy would have to wait. At mid-

Randy Johnson delivers a fireball against the Atlanta Braves in Game 1 of the 2001 National League Championship Series.

season he was dealt to Houston. Johnson won 10 straight games with four shutouts, but was beaten by San Diego's Kevin Brown in the playoffs. The Padres advanced to the World Series against New York.

One of the most coveted players in free-agent history, Johnson was signed to a four-year, $53 million deal by Arizona. He led the second-year franchise to the NL West title while joining Gaylord Perry and Pedro Martinez as the only pitchers to win Cy Young Awards in both leagues. He finished 17–9 with a 2.48 ERA, leading both leagues with 364 strikeouts, 12 complete games, and 271⅔ innings pitched.

Johnson, however, continued to fail in the playoffs. After losing Game 1 to the New York Mets in the NLDS, he tied a major league record with six consecutive postseason losses.

In April 2000 he tied the modern record with six victories. Leading the league in strikeouts (347) and winning percentage, Johnson earned Cy Young Award number three, becoming the third National League pitcher to win the trophy in consecutive seasons.

TRIVIA

Has Randy Johnson ever pitched a no-hit game?

Answers to the trivia questions are on pages 159–160.

The addition of Curt Schilling, however, did not help Arizona reach the postseason. Johnson achieved his 3,000th career strikeout that season, and in 2001 he started things off with another hot streak, recording 20 strikeouts in nine innings against the Cincinnati Reds on May 8. That tied the big-league record held by Roger Clemens and Kerry Wood. The old record had been held by Johnson's idols: Carlton, Seaver, and Ryan (19 each).

On July 19, 2001, Johnson set another record. The previous night's game against the Padres was delayed by two electrical explosions, knocking out a light tower in Qualcomm Stadium. When the game resumed the following day, Johnson replaced original starter Schilling in the top of the third. He pitched the next seven innings, striking out 16 Padres, breaking the record for strikeouts in a relief appearance, set 88 years earlier by Walter Johnson.

Randy Johnson was 21–6 with a 2.49 ERA and 372 strikeouts (just 11 shy of Ryan's single-season record of 383) in 249⅔ innings in 2001. In the postseason, he was brilliant, completely erasing the "loser" tag hung around his playoff reputation since his performance versus New York in 1995. The tandem of Schilling and Johnson has been called the best righty-lefty combo ever, which is a major statement considering the accomplishments of Christy Mathewson and Rube Marquard; Don Drysdale and Sandy Koufax; Jim Palmer and Dave McNally; Catfish Hunter and Vida Blue; Greg Maddux and Tom Glavine. They were co-MVPs of the unbelievable 2001 World Series.

He beat Atlanta 2–0 in the opener of the NLCS. In the World Series, Johnson hurled a three-hit shutout at Chase Field against the Yankees. In Game 6 he won 15–2, then earned the relief win in Game 7. Johnson won his third consecutive Cy Young Award—his fourth overall—a few weeks later.

In 2002 Johnson may have been even better: 24–5 with a 2.32 ERA and 334 strikeouts in 260 innings. His totals over four straight 300-strikeout seasons were 364 (1999), 347 (2000), 372 (2001), and 334 (2002). By 2002, he had won four straight Cy Young Awards and had pitched in numerous All-Star Games.

In a spring training game, Johnson threw a pitch that *killed a bird*, a fluke occurrence that somehow seems would not have happened to a pitcher who did not throw as hard, or release the ball as close to the plate, as Johnson.

As of this writing, he toils for the New York Yankees, where age has demonstrated that he's no longer as dominant as in his prime, yet he remains the best pitcher on their staff. His next goal: 300 career wins. Five years after retirement, Johnson is a lock for the Hall of Fame. When baseball pundits discuss the best southpaws ever—Lefty Grove, Warren Spahn, Sandy Koufax, Steve Carlton—his name will be right there with them.

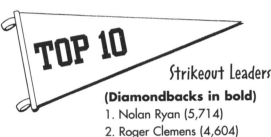

TOP 10

Strikeout Leaders

(Diamondbacks in bold)

1. Nolan Ryan (5,714)
2. Roger Clemens (4,604)
3. **Randy Johnson (4,544)**
4. Steve Carlton (4,136)
5. Bert Blyleven (3,701)
6. Tom Seaver (3,640)
7. Don Sutton (3,574)
8. Gaylord Perry (3,534)
9. Walter Johnson (3,509)
10. Phil Niekro (3,342)

Amazing Gracie

The Diamondbacks were a team assembled with "good character," considered by Colangelo, Garagiola, and Buck Showalter to be the primary ingredients of success. Nobody would say that Mark Grace lacks good character, but he definitely *is* a character.

Born in 1964, Mark Grace was a star at Tustin High School, in the shadow of Anaheim Stadium. Only a 24th-round pick in the 1985 draft, he came up to the major leagues in 1988 with the Chicago Cubs. The stereotype he had to overcome was that of the line drive–hitting first sacker. He played a position usually reserved for sluggers, and at Wrigley Field the need for power was paramount.

Grace was *The Sporting News* NL Rookie of the Year in 1988, hitting .296 with seven homers and 57 RBIs in 486 at-bats. He tied for the National League lead in errors by a first baseman in 1989, the year the Cubs captured the East Division crown but lost to Will Clark and San Francisco in the Championship Series. But Grace became a great defensive first sacker, earning Gold Gloves in 1992, 1993, 1995, and 1996.

He was an All-Star in 1993, 1995, and 1997. In that 1989 division title season, he hit .314, led the Cubs with 79 RBIs, and had 8 RBIs to go with a .647 batting average in the playoffs against the Giants.

Grace spent 11 more seasons with the Cubs, a team that took years to get back to their 1989 success. When pitcher Greg Maddux left as a free agent after the 1992 season, they were also-rans. Chicago finally reached the postseason again as a wild-card team

TRIVIA

When Mark Grace played at the AT&T Pebble Beach National Pro-Am golf tournament, who was he teamed up with?

Answers to the trivia questions are on pages 159–160.

Mark Grace smacks a two-run single in the sixth inning against his old team, the Chicago Cubs, in a May 2001 game in Chicago. It was Grace's first game at Wrigley Field since leaving the team in 2000 to join the Diamondbacks.

That Mark Grace went to San Diego State, the same school that produced his predecessor, Travis Lee?

in 1998, the year teammate Sammy Sosa slugged 66 homers. Grace hit 17 home runs that season. He consistently hit over .300 with the exception of 1991 (.273) and 1994 (.298).

Between 1990 and 1999, he had more hits as well as more doubles than any player. On August 2, 1999, Grace lined his 2,000th hit—a double—off Dustin Hermanson of the Expos.

Grace's teammates in Chicago included Ryne Sandberg, Andre Dawson, and Sosa. They tended to get more press attention. Certainly, the club had its share of offensive talent, but Maddux's absence left a hole in the pitching staff. The emergence of Kerry Wood in 1998 seemed to fill it, but as if living up to the "Cubbie curse," Wood suffered injuries that reduced his prodigious talents.

In 1992 Grace stated that he didn't "really want to become a guy that gets a lot of attention...I just want to be able to blend in." Chicago fans are among the most knowledgeable and appreciative in the country. They loved his work ethic in all phases of the game. Grace showed himself to be a "pro's pro." In a 1998 marketing promotion for Beanie Babies, they gave away "Gracie the Swan" in honor of the first baseman.

Grace wanted to play for a champion. In the last year of his contract (2000), he decided to make the move. After breaking a finger and tearing a hamstring in the spring, Grace was limited to just 34 games through April and May. Later in the season, Cubs' president and GM Andy MacPhail made it clear that Grace would not be re-signed. In the final week of the 2000 season, the press lobbied for him to stay. Fans produced signs imploring the club and Grace to come to terms.

Grace signed a two-year contract with Arizona. Recovered from his injury, he batted .298 with 78 RBIs while helping the D'backs to champion status. Winning the Series was "definitely the highest point of my life, especially for a lot of guys this late in their careers," he said. "If I step off a curb tomorrow and get hit by a car, truck, or bus, I'll die a happy man. Winning a ring is so important. I could retire today. Now I've accomplished everything I ever wanted in baseball."

Christian Soldier

Reggie Sanders was born in 1967. He and his wife, Wyndee, have three children. They make their home in Atlanta.

"I grew up in South Carolina, so the Braves were on TV all the time," he said. "Dale Murphy [a D'backs coach in 2001] was my hero. He hit home runs. He was just a big guy that had a lot of power. He and Bob Horner were the two guys I liked the most, but Dale Murphy was my main guy. I liked the way he hit home runs and the way he always battled back when he wasn't swinging the bat well. I met him when I was in Atlanta. It was pretty cool."

He also appreciated the Christianity of Murphy, a Mormon.

Sanders came out of Wilson High in Florence, South Carolina, and played at Spartanburg Methodist College. He started at Billings of the Pioneer League in 1988. In 1990 he hit 17 homers for Cedar Rapids, and batted .315 at Chattanooga in 1991.

The 6'1", 186-pounder was a right-handed batter and thrower. Sanders started his big-league career in 1991 when the Reds called him up. He hit .200 in his debut season.

Sanders improved to .270 with 12 home runs in 1992. In 1993 he enjoyed an excellent season, slamming 20 homers, driving in 83, and batting .274 with 27 stolen bases. The following year he hit .262.

Sanders made the National League All-Star team in 1995 when he batted .306 with 28 home runs and 99 runs batted in with 36

By the NUMBERS

.304—Reggie Sanders's batting average in the 2001 World Series.

stolen bases. Injuries plagued him in 1996 when he batted .251 with only 33 RBIs. It was a difficult year for Sanders, who appeared on the verge of true stardom only to be set back. He produced in 1997 with 19 home runs, but did not regain his 1996 form. He had another so-so season (14 home runs) in 1998.

Sanders played for San Diego and Atlanta before taking his talents to Arizona. With the 1999 Padres, he hit 26 home runs with 72 RBIs and a .285 batting average. The club, having lost Kevin Brown to free agency, failed to repeat. Arizona ran away with the West. At Atlanta in 2000, he batted a mere .232, although he played for a winning team.

Before his move to the desert, 1995 was his best year. He had persistent back and leg problems for years. During his seven seasons with the Cincinnati Reds, he developed a reputation for refusing to play through injuries that other players might have ignored. Tired of the whispering behind his back, the speedy outfielder bounced around the league for a few years, providing leadoff spark for the 1999 Padres and the 2000 Braves. But with the Diamondbacks in 2001 he was much more than "speedy." He developed real power hitting at Chase Field, producing his first 30-plus homer season while handling all three outfield positions.

Sanders stole 36 bases with the Padres in 1999. In particular, he looked forward to swiping a base with Randy Johnson on the mound.

"I knew with that type of delivery," said Sanders, "I could go on his first move."

Perhaps that was because he got on base against the Unit so rarely. He once struck out four times in one game facing Johnson, so in 2001 he decided, "If you can't beat 'em, join 'em."

Sanders also recalled a funny story about Randy: "I think we were playing St. Louis. Randy Johnson hit a ball that was a double. He hit a line drive between right field and center field. He went around

DID YOU KNOW . . . That a sportswriter in San Francisco once asked Reggie Sanders, "Are you a born again opposite field hitter?" Sanders replied, "I'm a born again Christian."

first base, tripped, and fell flat on his face. He had to go back to the base. So the next day they drew an outline of Randy's body right there at first base like he was dead! No, we didn't do the police tape around the scene."

Reversal of Fortune

The D'backs came off the splendid 2001 campaign full of confidence. They were a veteran team but not an old one. There was reason to believe this club would keep winning, that they were a dynasty in the desert.

The top competition in the National League would come from within their division, where Dusty Baker's Giants, who had barely lost the division to Arizona in 2001, felt they had the right stuff.

San Francisco featured a strong pitching staff, headed by Jason Schmidt and Russ Ortiz, with fireballing reliever Robb Nen in the closer's role. Second baseman Jeff Kent had won the 2000 MVP award. Left fielder Barry Bonds was...words cannot describe how devastating he was at this point, the very height of his career. He had broken Mark McGwire's single-season home run record in 2001, slamming 73. He would not approach that figure in 2002, but he would lead the league in batting at .370. His on-base average, slugging percentage, and fear factor in terms of what he meant to his team's line-up and how he screwed up opposition strategy was off the charts.

Nevertheless, all of his star power had not gotten his team past Arizona the year before. The Diamondbacks had every right to feel they were Caesar's Legions. They came, they saw, and they had conquered Bonds and San Francisco, the always-strong Atlanta Braves, and finally the baseball version of ultimate American power: the Yankees.

It was with this sense of hubris that Bob Brenly's club entered the 2002 campaign. Everything seemed to go according to Hoyle, at least as far as the regular season was concerned. Their 98–64 record was a six-game improvement over the World Championship club of 2001. It was good for first place in the competitive West, where, again, Mr. Bonds stood astride the division like a baseball Colossus. But Arizona had what it took to overcome Bonds and the Giants again.

Entering the season, Schilling was no longer a question mark, he was a Phoenix deity. Johnson was taking orders for a sculptor to make his Cooperstown plaque. The bullpen, however, was sketchy. Byung-Hyun Kim spent the off-season in a religious shrine, giving thanks that his "blown by blown" saves of the 2001 World Series had, almost by miracle, not cost his team a pennant. His teammates saved his name from the Wall of Infamy alongside Fred Merkle, Fred Snodgrass, Ralph Branca, and Bill Buckner.

"Amazing Gracie" was hardly recognizable anymore. It was not just the fact that, in order to cover up his thinning hair, he shaved it all under the auspices that it was "in style." Yeah, sure it is. On the field, his .252 average demonstrated that his skills were heading where his hair already was: down the drain.

Rod Barajas sits dejected in the dugout following the Diamondbacks' loss to the St. Louis Cardinals by the score of 6–3 to clinch the National League Division series at Busch Stadium in October 2002.

IF ONLY . . . Arizona had won the 1999 World Series after winning 100 games, and the 2002 World Series after winning 98 games, the D'backs of this period would go down in history as one of the great short-term dynasties of all time.

Junior Spivey replaced Jay Bell, and from an offensive statistical point of view improved the spot with a .301 average to go with 78 RBIs. Tony Womack continued to be as consistent as a certain hot spring in Yellowstone Park, batting .271. Notre Dame's Craig Counsell, a key contributor in the Series, was spurred by success, hitting .282 and handling the defensive chores at the hot corner.

Gonzo settled into what certainly appeared to be his normal power range. His 28 home runs were less than half of his gaudy 2001 numbers. At .288 and 103 RBIs, he was still a top producer, although by 2002 baseball statistics were so skewed that 100-plus runs batted in did not look nearly so impressive as it did when guys named Yastrzemski or Jackson were doing it. Gonzo had done so much so fast that he may even have dreamed a little dream about Cooperstown, but that was a bit much. Steve Finley improved to .287 with 25 home runs and 89 RBIs. He began a run over the next years that established that his steady career record ultimately would prove better than Gonzalez's, his power more...realistic. Quinton McCracken batted .309. Damian Miller was good old Damian Miller.

David Dellucci, Matt Williams, Rod Barajas, Danny Bautista, Jose Guillen, Jay Bell, and Erubiel Durazo made up the reserves, as some of the old was being replaced by the new.

Johnson was out of his cotton-pickin' mind on the mound at 24–5 with a 2.32 ERA, which translated to 1966 or 1968 would probably have looked more like 30–4 with a 1.65 ERA and, say, 380 strikeouts give or take. On the pitcher's mound, it does not get any better.

Oh, wait, what about Schilling? Okay, just a smidgen's difference. Arguing who was better was splitting hairs: Churchill or Eisenhower? Lincoln or Washington? Just order the plaque for the Big Unit, and while you're at it, get one for Curt, too: 23–7 with a 3.23 ERA in an era in which 4.00 was the old 3.00. He just mowed 'em down. Eighty percent of pro athletes getting paid the kind of dough he got that year ($10 million) would have had the work ethic of communist factory hands, but Schilling turned it on so high steam was coming out of his ears.

Baseball fans in the Valley of the Sun, who had of course seen spring training ball for decades but regular-season action just a few years, stared in awe and wonder. In front of their eyes was pitching dominance of the rarest quality. They ate it up with a spoon, as appreciative as orphaned kids getting their first Christmas presents.

Of course the drop off after those two again looked look like the waterfall scene from *Butch Cassidy and the Sundance Kid*, but it was enough to get to those 98 wins. Rick Helling, once an All-American at Stanford—one of those kids who won 20 games at Texas when his team won every game 10–6—managed a creditable 10–12 mark with a 4.51 ERA. Miguel Batista, when not quoting Shakespeare or offering his views on how life after death can be explained by quantum physics, was 8–9. Brian Anderson was Brian Anderson.

Mike Myers was on the team for one reason: to pitch to Bonds, which he did fairly effectively with his submarine left-handed offerings. Kim somehow had amnesia, forgetting 2001 and coming through with a huge season. He earned 36 saves with a sterling 2.04 ERA.

Greg Swindell was on his last legs, the highlight of the season coming for him when his alma mater, Texas, won the College World Series. Mike Morgan kept the clubhouse loose telling stories about drinking with Babe Ruth.

By August 1 they were 65–43 with no looking back. Four days later, Johnson (15–4) shut out the Mets 2–0 at Shea Stadium. According to rumor, proctologists were needed for New York bat removals. On August 11 at home, Schilling won number 19 over talented Josh Beckett 9–2.

TRIVIA

Who did the Diamondbacks play in the first round of the 2002 National League playoffs?

Answers to the trivia questions are on pages 159–160.

Johnson and Schilling developed the reputations of the only two pitchers in the game who challenged Barry Bonds, *and they usually came out ahead.* Telling a pitcher to stop Barry Bonds in 2002 was like Hitler telling his Wehrmacht commanders, "Your orders are to stop Patton when he gets to the Saar."

The Hero

Curt Schilling is a hero. He loves his country, he is smart, and he's a family man who represents precisely what a professional athlete should.

Schilling is a military historian. Had he not been blessed with extraordinary baseball ability, he would have entered the military, like his brother, Captain Dan Schilling. He was one of the featured army heroes of the book, documentary, and film *Black Hawk Down*. Since that 1993 battle in Mogadishu, Somalia, Captain Schilling has continued to be a daredevil parachutist. He is Curt's hero.

The big question about Schilling is whether he will go into the Baseball Hall of Fame. In 2006 he passed 200 career victories, but his career regular-season record is by no means that of a sure Cooperstown inductee like Randy Johnson. Schilling was utterly dominant in 2001 and 2002, but Steve Stone was utterly dominant in 1980; Orel Hershiser was in 1988; Dean Chance in 1964. Those guys will not get into the Hall of Fame.

Schilling's prospects hinge on several factors. First, he is a World Series hero, a clutch October pitcher whose record as of this writing approaches that of Bob Gibson and Catfish Hunter. This is rare air.

Next is the question of what he will do beyond the date of this writing. He could add to his October legend. He also could pitch long enough to rack up a significant number of career victories. If he can get up to 230 or 240 wins, it will make his case a better one.

But what truly makes Schilling so special is what he did in 2004 with the Boston Red Sox. He would be the first to say that all he did was pitch baseball games, albeit with an ankle injury that caused blood to soak his *red* sock. (Various pissants of low order have attempted to put forth the fiction that Schilling painted his sock for shock value.)

Schilling would point out that real heroes do the things his brother did in Somalia, but when it comes to baseball dramatics, considering all the circumstances, Schilling rates at the very top. He is below Lou Gehrig's "luckiest man on the face of the Earth" speech, but who isn't?

Schilling took Boston on his back, leading the most cursed, psychologically impaired franchise and fans to the Promised Land. It was so big in Boston, and such a marvel of baseball drama, that it may just get Schilling into the Hall.

Born in 1966, Schilling graduated from Shadow Mountain High School in Phoenix in 1985. He then helped pitch Yavapai Junior College to the JUCO World Series before getting drafted in the second round by Boston in 1986.

The 6'4", 215-pound right-hander struggled through the Boston, Baltimore, and Houston organizations. In 1990 the great Roger Clemens sought him out. Clemens told him he had been watching him and recognized that he possessed great potential, but unless Curt became more dedicated to the game, his talent would be wasted.

Schilling took Clemens's advice to heart. After a trade to Philadelphia, he started to find himself. In 1993 he led a gritty, underdog Phillies club to an improbable victory over the powerhouse Braves in the National League Championship Series. He defeated Toronto in the World Series, but the Blue Jays won a thrilling fall classic.

Injuries stopped Schilling cold in the mid-1990s, but he regained his stuff with a 17-win season in 1997 and a 15–6 mark in 1999. Schilling also became, almost overnight, a devastating strikeout artist. He struck out 319 hitters in 1997 and 300 in 1999.

His statistics and sudden emergence as a fastball pitcher look suspicious on paper. The "steroid era" was in full swing by the late

DID YOU KNOW . . . That Curt Schilling was honored as Phi Delta Theta's Lou Gehrig Award winner in 1996? The award is presented annually to the major league player who best exemplifies the giving character of fraternity brother Lou Gehrig.

Curt Schilling winds up on the strikeout pitch to Milwaukee's Jorge Fabregas in the eighth inning of a September 2002 game. Schilling and Randy Johnson became the first teammates to surpass the 300-strikeout mark in one season.

1990s. In recent years it has been revealed that pitchers, not just hitters, used "juice." As is the case with Luis Gonzalez and other players, there is no evidence that Schilling juiced, but the shadow over the game is so large that, unfortunately, the suspicion is impossible to avoid.

That said, Schilling's body make-up never seemed to change. He is tall and has big legs and a perfect pitcher's body with impeccable mechanics. Most juicers became huge or their bodies took on a supertight quality. They also suffer a variety of strange injuries. This does not describe Schilling, who despite an excellent work ethic still has a slightly pudgy look to him.

Instead of steroids, it appears that Schilling simply mastered two elements of pitching. One, he developed a motion that was perfect for his body. Like Tom Seaver, whose physical type resembled Schilling's, he got maximum explosive power out of his over-the-top delivery. Two, Schilling is one of—if not the most—prepared pitchers in the game. (Barry Zito is the only other pitcher who matches his brainpower.) Schilling gets many strikeouts based on his knowledge of hitters, the strike zone, and a mental edge he maintains over batters. He and Johnson are two of the only pitchers who challenged Barry Bonds in his prime and succeeded.

Schilling's fastball is a wonder, but he does not throw as hard as Johnson or even Clemens in his best years. He did develop a nasty splitter and slider, two ultimate strikeout pitches.

Schilling also is an iron man who has gone the distance more often than any other pitcher since the game changed in the late 1970s. His competitive nature is perfectly harnessed with his intelligence. If one were to translate his on-field approach to combat, he would be considered an ideal field commander, capable of keeping a calm approach in the most trying of circumstances, just as Captain Schilling did when he and his Rangers fought their way out of Mogadishu in October 1993. That was the same month Curt was pitching in the World Series.

In 1999 his pregnant wife, Shonda, was hospitalized to treat a life-threatening blood clot. Scheduled to make his first start since shoulder surgery, Schilling prepared to go into the game until manager Terry Francona sent him home.

"As much as I would have liked to have him pitch," said Francona, "I told him I thought he might regret that later."

Schilling's wife successfully gave birth to their third child a few days later.

In 2001 Shonda was diagnosed with melanoma, a skin cancer. She required four months of surgery and treatment to send the disease into remission.

"Her battle hasn't made me a better pitcher," he said, "but it's made me a better person, I hope, and a better husband and father." That season, he won more than 20 games for the first time en route to an Arizona world championship.

TRIVIA

What did Curt Schilling name his two sons?

Answers to the trivia questions are on pages 159–160.

Shonda's diagnosis was a wake-up call for Schilling, since he had overcome an addiction to chewing tobacco. His father, a chronic smoker, died of lung cancer when Schilling was 10. After the birth of Schilling's first child, he decided he didn't want to repeat family history and attempted to quit chewing tobacco before spring training in 1995.

"I quit cold turkey one time and for two weeks," he told *Baseball Weekly*. "I couldn't believe I had done it. I was feeling okay and then one night I got violently ill. I threw up all night, headaches, sweating, everything."

He relapsed. In 1998 he had a white lesion removed from his jaw, but chewed again in 2000 when he accepted a golf buddy's offer of just one "dip." He has fought the addiction successfully in the years since.

After September 11, 2001, he wrote an open letter to baseball fans, saying, "Please know that athletes in this country look to your husbands and wives as they may have looked at the men of our profession when they were young, as heroes, as idols, for they are everything every man should strive to be in life and they died in a way reserved only for those who would make the ultimate sacrifice for this nation, and for the freedom we oftentimes take for granted."

Either Schilling or Greg Maddux started the practice of covering their mouths when talking to catchers and managers on the mound, knowing a lip-reader watching on a clubhouse TV could use the words against him. Schilling says Phillies catcher Darren Daulton suggested it to him during the 1993 World Series.

Schilling was named the championship series MVP in 1993. In 1997 he fanned 15 batters in one game. Also in 1997 he struck out 16 Yankees. Later that year, he retired the first 22 batters he faced. He passed the 300-strikeout mark in that game. In September 1997 Schilling broke J. R. Richard's National League mark for strikeouts by a right-handed pitcher, a record held previously by Tom Seaver, who broke his own record in 1971. Schilling's back-to-back 300-strikeout seasons of 1997 and 1998 were a rarity in baseball. In 1998 Schilling struck out 15 to beat Greg Maddux 2–1, and later that August he threw his major league–leading 13th complete game.

In 2001, with Arizona, Schilling was 22–6 with a 2.98 ERA and 293 strikeouts in 256⅔ innings. He was dominant in postseason play, beating the Yankees 9–1 at home, leaving with a 1–1 tie after seven at Yankee Stadium in a game Byung-Hyun Kim blew; then matching Roger Clemens in an amazing Game 7 won by the D'backs in Phoenix. He and Johnson were co-MVPs of the Series as well as co-Sportsmen of the Year by *Sports Illustrated*. In 2002 he was 23–7 with a 3.23 ERA, with 316 strikeouts in 259⅓ innings.

Schilling's 2004 exploits earned him a second Sportsman of the Year honor. With the Red Sox in that charmed campaign, Schilling was 21–6 with a 3.26 ERA pitching in front of Fenway Park's Green Monster. In the playoffs, Boston rebounded from down three games to none to beat the hated Yankees in New York.

ALL-DECADE TEAM

2000s All-Decade Diamondbacks Team

Position	Name
Pitcher	Curt Schilling
Pitcher	Randy Johnson
Pitcher	Miguel Batista
Pitcher	Brandon Webb
Catcher	Damian Miller
First Base	Mark Grace
Second Base	Jay Bell
Third Base	Matt Williams
Short Stop	Tony Womack
Outfield	Luis Gonzalez
Outfield	Steve Finley
Outfield	Reggie Sanders
Manager	Bob Brenly

Boston won the game, but Schilling had injured his ankle. Team doctors had to suture his tendon to his skin to prevent further damage, allowing him to pitch and win one of the most memorable games in the national pastime's long history. Schilling's performance has few equals in sports annals. It earned him stature in Beantown short of John Kennedy, but up there with Ted Williams, Carl Yastrzemski, Larry Bird, and Tom Brady. In the championship, he beat St. Louis 6–2, as Boston swept the series for their first World Series since 1918, ending the "Curse of the Bambino."

In 2006 Schilling was a leading candidate for the Cy Young Award until September, when he and the Sox tailed off. It is an award that has eluded him since his time in Arizona when he pitched alongside Randy Johnson.

The Philosopher

Miguel Batista came up to the major leagues with Pittsburgh in 1992, toiling in obscurity with Florida, the Chicago Cubs, Montreal, and Kansas City, before arriving in Phoenix. He pitched effectively in the 2001 World Series. With the media spotlight on him for he first time, it was his off-field interests that generated attention.

When the press came around to his locker stall, they noticed a photo of Albert Einstein, along with books of philosophy. Questioned, the Dominican native told people that Einstein was his biggest hero. He read voraciously and wrote poems on the side.

Before coming to the D'backs, Batista left the Expos organization three times—first as a Rule V selection by the Pirates in 1991, again when he was released by the club in 1994, and finally when a trade sent him to Kansas City for Brad Rigby in 2000.

In 1997 the Cubs obtained outfielder Henry Rodriguez from the Expos in exchange for Batista.

"Whoever has been surprised [by a trade] has not played for the Expos," Batista told the *Montreal Gazette* that April. "Either you're a superstar or a prospect, and I'm not any of those."

Kansas City manager Tony Muser was impressed with Batista, awarding him a spot in the starting rotation. Batista managed just one win and a 6.56 ERA in his next nine games. He returned to the bullpen, made only four inconsequential appearances, and was designated for assignment in late June before finishing the season at Triple-A Omaha.

TRIVIA

Miguel Batista hails from Santo Domingo, Dominican Republic. Why is the Dominican such a hotbed of baseball talent?

Answers to the trivia questions are on pages 159–160.

Miguel Batista follows through on a pitch against the Los Angeles Dodgers during the first inning of an August 2002 game.

In 2001 and now with Arizona, Batista had an 11–8 record with a 3.36 ERA. He was injured early on, but recovered. Batista got the 5–3 win when Arizona took a 2–1 lead in its division series victory over St. Louis.

In 2002 Batista hurled nine innings of one-hit ball against the Giants, but San Francisco won 1–0 in 10 innings. The 6'0", 160-pound Batista could relieve as well as start.

"I never even played baseball until I was 15 years old," he said. "I was always doing gymnastics and basketball, and we played stickball in the street. I never had a high school coach, only a physical education teacher. So the only hero I ever had when I was little was my grandmother. She was my hero and she still is my hero. I never wanted to 'be like Mike' or like Babe Ruth. I only wanted to be like my grandmother. She's the greatest human being I've ever seen. The current player I really admire is Moises Alou. Some people say to me, 'Well, that's just because he's another Dominican.' It's not because he's Dominican. He's the most consistent hitter I've ever seen."

Born in 1971, he attends museums on the road.

"I don't really look at him as a scientist," he said of his Einstein fixation. "I'm more interested in some of the other stuff he talked about: the imagination and even his theories about life after death."

Batista claims not to be religious, but rather feels that "life forces" and "energy" transfers from one place to another, ideas he says were Einstein's. "I say the same thing that Mahatma Gandhi said: 'My only religion is love,'" said Batista.

Batista, like other intellectual ballplayers, was viewed curiously within the confines of baseball thinking, but society has changed over the years. The game is not as closed-minded as it once was. Still, he was considered a loner, but he professed no problem with that.

"I found something more fulfilling than baseball," he said. "The searching of the truth—this is something that, for me, is more important than anything in the world."

Batista is also musically inclined and a movie buff. While some might feel his future could be political, or in education, he maintained simple goals.

"What do I see myself doing 30 years from now?" he asked. "Probably riding and raising animals. I like that. I would like to have a farm and raise animals. I had too many of them and had to let them go."

Maybe his next book should be George Orwell's *Animal Farm*.

By the NUMBERS   **0.00**—Miguel Batista's ERA over two games and eight innings in the 2001 World Series.

Byung-Hyun Kim

When comparing great baseball players over the eras, it is often said that those who performed after the color barrier was broken by Jackie Robinson rate a slight edge because they faced a wider range of competition.

Over time, Latin players made an enormous impact on the game. But in the 1990s baseball became truly internationalized. The game became an official Olympic sport, cable and satellite television brought it to all four corners of the globe, and as a result superstars from Asia came to play in the U.S.

Baseball became popular in Italy, Australia, Canada, and the Netherlands, but it was always a huge sport in Asia. Japan is nothing less than *gaga* about baseball, but it is a way of life in Taiwan and South Korea, too.

Some have argued that expansion has diluted the talent base, but this is not true. The talent base has expanded. Expansion has simply accommodated that talent base. There has been a vast improvement in amateur baseball—little leagues, high schools, American Legion, travel ball. Of course the college baseball experience, which consists of a year-round regimen in the fall, the spring schedule, and collegiate summer leagues in Alaska, Cape Cod, and others, creates far better players than in the past.

On top of all this, economics, training methods, diet, coaching, and weight-training have improved the athletes. There is no doubt that the modern baseball player is, on the whole, better than ever, regardless of the nostalgia for the past. Unfortunately, the competition to get there, to stay there, and to thrive there, has directly resulted in steroid abuse. The worst truth about steroids is that it

13.50—Byung-Hyun Kim's ERA over three and one-third innings in the 2001 World Series.

unquestionably improves performance, making it an irresistible temptation.

Japanese players first came to play for the Giants in the 1960s, but it was Hideo Nomo who opened doors for Asians in the 1990s. That was the door Byung-Hyun Kim walked through.

What made Kim unusual was the fact he first signed a pro baseball contract with an American team. Unlike Nomo, Ichiro Suzuki, and others, he was not an established professional star in his native country.

Kim was a college sophomore in South Korea when he signed with the Diamondbacks in 1999. Before that, he defeated the vaunted Cubans in the 1997 Four Nations Invitational Games in Osaka, Japan. He was a member of the Korean National team, where he attracted great attention by fanning 15 U.S. Olympic hitters in a game in Tucson in 1998. From there, he accompanied his team to Italy for the world championships, where he earned a save—again versus the U.S.—in the championship game.

He led South Korea to a gold medal in the Asian Games, fanning 12 against China with eight straight strikeouts. His work in international competition earned him a contract from the Diamondbacks, as well as a deferment from the South Korean army.

Employing a variety of side-arm and under-hand deliveries to the plate, Kim overpowered hitters with a fiendish collection of fastballs, sliders, and curves that seemingly obeyed no known laws of physics. His phenomenal strikeout totals earned the 5'11" right-hander the nickname "the Little Unit," a nod to his 6'10" teammate and fellow strikeout master Randy Johnson, the Big Unit.

Kim was the youngest player in the majors when the Diamondbacks brought him up from Double-A El Paso in May 1999. At first, he looked actually unhittable with his side delivery. The initial reaction to him was one of wonder. Sports talk host Jim Rome got wind of him and raved. He reminded people of the mythological Sidd Finch, a *Sports Illustrated* "story" about a 120-mile an hour wunderkind who could not be hit.

"I don't know how he does it," said D'backs third baseman Matt Williams after watching his new teammate demonstrate his assortment of gravity-defying sliders. "He's got one that drops and one that rises. He's amphibious."

Eventually, Kim was revealed to be a human being, not a strikeout machine, but hopes were high for him. Buck Showalter went to him on May 29 at Shea Stadium. Brought in to pitch the bottom of the ninth with the Diamondbacks clinging to an 8–7 lead, Kim retired Edgardo Alfonzo and John Olerud before fanning Mike Piazza to end the game.

He pitched sporadically after that, however. In retrospect, Kim might have benefited from more minor league seasoning than 10 games in El Paso, 11 in Tucson, and one in the Arizona Rookie League.

In 2000, when Arizona stopper Matt Mantei opened the season on the disabled list, he was put into the closer's role for much of the first half. Kim (or B.K. as his teammates called him) was almost untouchable. On two separate occasions, he struck out eight consecutive batters over a three-game or four-game stretch. He whiffed 11 out of 12 batters over five games. For the year, he struck out 111 hitters in just 70⅔ innings, or more than 14 per nine innings.

Kim struggled in 2000. He was considered All-Star material with his 14 saves and 1.82 ERA over his initial 28 appearances, but slumped enough to "earn" an option back to Triple-A Tucson on July 30. During his stay in Tucson, Kim was used as a starter in an effort to restore his confidence and improve his mechanics, particularly his slow delivery from the stretch. With Mantei reestablished as the club's closer, Kim pitched as a setup man when the club recalled him in August. He even started a game for Arizona after 84 relief appearances, allowing four runs in a two-and-one-third-inning no-decision on September 26 at Colorado's Coors Field.

Eventually Kim took over the closer's role when Mantei was lost to torn elbow ligaments. Kim shared duties with rookie Bret Prinz at first, but by the end of 2001, the job was his.

On September 18, the Rockies came back from a 6–0 deficit in the first inning, pounding Curt Schilling to defeat the Diamondbacks 10–9. The Rockies won it on dramatic back-to-back homers by Todd Helton and Jeff Cirillo off Kim.

Byung-Hyun Kim fires away during the Diamondbacks' last spring training game in March 2003.

This game may have affected Kim. The language differential made it difficult for people to understand what he was going through, but more than that, cultural differences as it related to sports increased his problems.

The American philosophy to baseball, particularly at the professional level in which teams play 162-game schedules, is one of a calm approach. It can be compared to the even keel attitude of test pilots, who, despite high casualty rates in which their comrades periodically are killed, nevertheless maintain a calm demeanor because getting upset would negatively affect their flying.

This uniquely American attitude is different from other countries. European and Latin American soccer is performed in a kamikaze manner, each play agonized over; wild gesticulations,

Most Disastrous Home Run Allowed in World Series Play
(Diamondbacks in bold)

1. Mitch Williams to Joe Carter, 1992
2. Ralph Terry to Bill Mazeroski, 1960
3. Dennis Eckersley to Kirk Gibson, 1988
4. **Byung-Hyun Kim to Derek Jeter, 2001**
5. Charlie Root to Babe Ruth, 1932
6. Mike Marshall to Joe Rudi, 1974
7. Charlie Hough to Reggie Jackson, 1977
8. **Byung-Hyun Kim to Tino Martinez, 2001**
9. Rawly Eastwick to Bernie Carbo, 1975
10. Rube Marquard to Home Run Baker, 1911

pained facial expressions, huge celebrations. Baseball, as opposed to football, produces the more day-by-day approach. An individual football game, particularly in college where a single loss can eliminate a team's national championship aspirations, takes on titanic meaning.

It is a bit odd that baseball took the way it did in Asia. Despite the long schedules, the ups and downs of a season, the inevitable slumps of this crazy "game of failure," the mindset of "face" and "honor" and "shame" contributes to a fanatical fan base. Players take an almost life or death approach to each game, starting at the beginning of the year until the last game is over.

A player brings honor or shame to his team, his village, and his family with each successful or unsuccessful outing. It's a tough way to live, but it's the way they've done it for centuries. It is also the worst *possible* mindset for a closer.

The average American relief pitcher might give up a game-winning home run and be seen that night whooping it up with a few cold beers. While this can be disconcerting, causing some to believe he doesn't care, it's the best way to handle failure. He must have amnesia. He must forget his failures. He must live to fight another day.

Each pitcher handles it differently.

"Dennis Eckersley was scared to death of failure," A's announcer Bill King said in 2001. "That's what drove him."

Then there was another A's relief ace, Rollie Fingers.

"Rollie was too dumb to know any better," said former teammate Rick Monday. "He'd be on the mound, bases loaded, full count. Somebody else would be afraid to walk the guy in and groove one for a homer. Rollie'd throw that yak slider on the outside black for strike three. Nothing fazed him."

Getting hit—losing face in the eyes of his teammates, the fans, the world—*fazed* Byung-Hyun Kim. Big time.

On October 31, 2001, in one of the most exciting games ever played at Yankee Stadium, the Yankees defeated the Diamondbacks 4–3 in 10 innings to tie the Series at two games apiece. Tino Martinez's two-out, two-run home run in the bottom of the ninth tied the game. Derek Jeter's blast in the bottom of the tenth won it for New York. Both homers came off Byung-Hyun Kim, who blew Curt Schilling's lead, then the game.

That was just the first night.

On November 1, history repeated itself. The Yankees came from two runs down with two outs in the ninth inning to defeat the Diamondbacks 3–2 in 12 innings. Kim was the victim of Scott Brosius's two-run home run in the ninth. Alfonso Soriano's single won it in the twelfth.

TRIVIA

Byung-Hyun Kim is from Asia. Why is baseball so popular there?

Answers to the trivia questions are on pages 159–160.

A Shifting Desert Wind

All good things come to an end. In sports, dynasties are made out of teams that can transition from old to new, continuing to remain victorious. This has marked Yankees greatness over the decades. The Montreal Canadiens, Notre Dame Fighting Irish, Boston Celtics; these are among the traditions separating themselves from the good, entering into another realm.

There is no greater challenge for a coach, manager, GM, or owner. Money must be spent well. Wise decisions must be accompanied by good luck, which as Branch Rickey once said is "the residue of design."

The 2003 Diamondbacks were by no means a disaster. In some ways they were a victim of their own success and of changing times. They certainly cannot be compared to the 1998 and 2004 Florida Marlins, both defending world champions who had no second act.

The D'backs were a veteran club. In order to maintain their level of success, they counted on stars to perform at their expected high level. Players of a certain age had to stay "young" rather than get "old."

Their 84–78 mark, good for third place in the West, reflected the fact that there was still enough talent to have a winning record but not enough to withstand injuries and age.

The reserves tell the story. Tony Womack (.237), Raul Mondesi (22 RBIs), Mark Grace (.200), and Matt Williams (.246) were All-Stars or close to it at one point. Each was over the hill by 2004, like rock stars who had lost their young audience; hot actors whose style was now laughed at by the young girls who swooned to them in days of yore.

Mark Grace salutes fans as he leaves the field for the last time as a player in a September 2003 game against the St. Louis Cardinals.

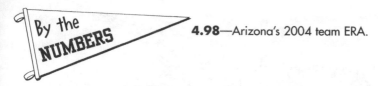

4.98—Arizona's 2004 team ERA.

The Yankees replaced a Phil Rizzuto with a Tony Kubek, a Yogi Berra with an Elston Howard. The Celtics had a John Havlicek and a Dave Cowens to step in for a K. C. Jones and a Bill Russell. These are exceptions to the rule. Joe Garagiola Jr. surely knew the formula, but the ingredients to conjure it up are like precious oil. You drill and drill and drill, usually coming up dry.

So it was that Lyle Overbay with his .276 average had to endure the painful truth that, try as he might, he was no Mark Grace. Craig Counsell, a utilityman, a clutch player in the 2001 World Series, a proud Golden Domer, nevertheless went to work each day living amidst the silent truth that he could not hold a candle to Matt Williams in his prime.

Junior Spivey hustled, hit .255, tried hard, but made nobody forget the deeds of Jay Bell from a few seasons before. Rod Barajas became a fan favorite—an earnest .218-hitting fan favorite. Damian Miller had never reminded anybody of Johnny Bench or Roy Campanella, but he did not hit .218 in the championship years, either. Danny Bautista hit his .275 with virtually no power.

There were some bright spots. Luis Gonzalez produced. True, his 26 home runs looked miniscule next to his Foxxian production of two years' prior, but at .304 with 104 runs batted in, nobody was going to find much fault with Gonzo. He remained the best of the good guys. Steve Finley continued to prove his consistency with 22 longballs to go with a creditable .287 average, great defense, good speed, and leadership.

Truth be told, the '03 D'backs could have won the pennant with the offense they produced, but only if the pitching held up. It did not. Curt Schilling had a problem with run support, as his 8–9 record with a 2.95 ERA suggests, but he was not as dominant as he had been. He was no spring chicken anymore. Had he run his course? The Phoenix native and his $10 million salary were on the way out. When Boston picked him up, it looked like a desperate move by the "cursed" Bosox.

Randy Johnson suffered injuries. The D'backs had no chance whatsoever of fashioning greatness out of a season in which the Unit posted a 6–8 record with a 4.26 ERA. It was as if the Union Army had cut a swath through Georgia only to have Florida beat them to win the Civil War.

Still, there were good signs. Young Brandon Webb was 10–9 with an outstanding 2.84 ERA. Miguel Batista was never going to be a guy who reminded anybody of Jim Bunning, but he was by now a proven, effective major league hurler, as his 10–9 record with a 3.54 ERA attested to. Elmer Dessens was 8–8.

Matt Mantei was terrific, earning 29 saves with a 2.62 ERA. Oscar Villarreal posted a 10–7 mark. Mike Myers continued to send thank you notes to Barry Bonds for providing him a job in baseball. Stephen Randolph was 8–1.

It was the Giants' year. San Francisco had come *this close* to beating Anaheim in the 2002 World Series, a duel between wild-card survivors. Bonds's performance did not drop off at all in 2003. He was the MVP for the third straight time, powering his team to the play-offs. There was no last line of defense in Arizona; no Galahads of the mound in the form of Johnson and Schilling to ward off this Barbarian from the West, who finally stormed the gates and sacked the city.

It fell to the sturdy right arm of Florida's Josh Beckett to stop the Giants in the playoffs, then to put on a pitching clinic at Yankee Stadium, enshrining his name in the annals of Series glory.

Oh, but 2003 looked like a season to remember compared with 2004. Arizona fans, the sophisticated, savvy, business-friendly citizens of a "City of the Future," were shocked to discover that mediocrity existed in their midst. They had a plan, a winning formula, but now it was back to the drawing board. They had been spoiled like trust fund kids, but now they got a taste of what it was like in K.C., Milwaukee, and Chicago for 100 years.

Their 51–111 record landed them fifth in the division. They scored 615 runs, allowed 899. Bob Brenly and his laissez-faire style suddenly looked hugely unpopular.

Arizona drew 2,519,560, a figure that at one time would mean champagne in the streets. But baseball had changed. It was a corporate sport, run by billionaires, played by multimillionaires, watched by business tycoons in luxury boxes. It was certainly more popular in terms of attendance, TV ratings, and merchandising than it ever had been in its history, but the bottom line was now sky high.

TRIVIA

How many MVP awards have been won by Arizona State Sun Devils?

Answers to the trivia questions are on pages 159–160.

Individual baseball games now took on the nightly show biz atmosphere of a single pro football game. The concept of selling out *every single game*, which would have drawn laughter in the 1970s, was now a reality in San Francisco, New York, Boston, Phoenix. The D'backs' attendance fell far short of that standard, placing them eighth out of 16 National League franchises.

This was a team with a bunch of guys named Juan Brito, Shea Hillenbrand, Scott Hairston, Chad Tracy, and Alex Cintron. Gonzo and Finley performed like the old pros they were, but there was no supporting cast. Roberto Alomar came on board, but his game was a shadow of its old self.

Randy Johnson was 16–14, a Herculean effort on a 111-loss team. Brandon Webb's production dropped, and after that it was just a cast of castoffs.

Crossroads

The 2004 season was the low point in the short, ultimately wonderful history of the Arizona Diamondbacks. A model baseball organization in every way had experienced real failure for the first time. A challenge was posed. Would it be met?

In that 2004 campaign, Diamondbacks supporters and fans throughout Baseball Land watched in awe as Curt Schilling put on an unreal display of pitching guts and greatness. Boston won the World Series, which was worthy of headlines resembling something just smaller than Living Christ Returns to Jerusalem!

In 2005 Randy Johnson, who had once pined for Arizona, bought a home in Paradise Valley, raised his kids there; took off for New York, New York.

In San Francisco, it all fell like a house of cards on Barry Bonds. After winning his fourth straight MVP in 2004 (seventh overall), a series of accusations, revelations, indictments, books, and subpoenas reigned on him like Russian artillery shells exploding around Hitler's bunker. His place in baseball history, his reputation as a man and player, dropped like stocks bought on margin in 1929. The Giants blew the 2004 division to L.A. on the last day in a reversal of fortune, Bobby Thomson–style, with the Dodgers' *Steve Finley* wearing the hero's mantle. In 2005 Bonds was hurt most of the year, slowing down his chase of Babe Ruth's and Hank Aaron's records.

The division became a wide-open one throughout 2005 and 2006, but nobody seemed willing to step up and take it. Pundits called it the "National League Worst." In Arizona, a sign of the times came in the form of new general partner Jeff Moorad.

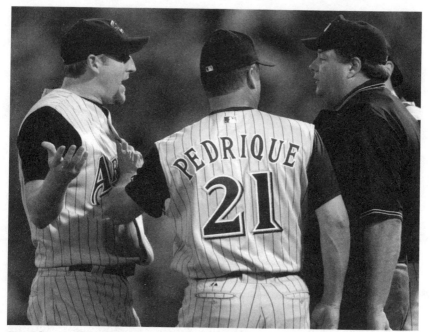

Brandon Webb is held back by his manager, Al Pedrique, during an argument with home plate umpire Jerry Layne in September 2004.

Moorad had been a junior partner of legendary sports agent Leigh Steinberg. He handled the baseball operations, with Steinberg specializing in football. One of Moorad's clients had been Al Martin, once a promising outfielder for the Pirates who maintained an off-season Scottsdale residence with his wife and family.

During the seasons Martin flew his mistress from city to city. Pirates wives got wind of their husbands' dalliances, calling up hotels for phone records for "tax purposes" to find out who was sleeping with whom and where. It could be argued that the explosion of cell phones is traced to the fallout of this event. Martin's career careened downward, as did his personal life. In the late 1990s he apparently got drunk and "married" one of his girlfriends in Las Vegas, even though he was still married to his wife. Waking up the next day, he tried to annul the Vegas union, but when the woman in question insisted on marriage and all the financial accoutrements that go with it, Martin pulled a gun, stuck it in her mouth, and told her, "I'll O.J. you." *Niiice.*

Baby-sitting men-children can get old. No doubt incidents such as this one put one too many gray hairs on Moorad's head, so he decided to take it to the next level: club ownership in the Diamondbacks. Walter O'Malley would have rolled over in his grave knowing an agent was now an owner, but the business had changed...into a business.

"I think the club has shown an awful lot in the couple of weeks closing out the season and really, I think, given all of us a confidence that we do have the right nucleus on the field," Moorad said of the 2005 Diamondbacks. "I think the goal at this point is to make some adjustments—certainly to tweak the roster a bit. But I'm not sure that wholesale changes are required. I think we'll certainly be open-minded about the free-agent market. I think the free-agent market is a thinner one than in years past, but again, we have some needs. We'd like to improve our production at the catcher position. We're committed to going into next season with as close to a bulletproof bullpen as we can get."

It was certainly a new roster. The last vestiges of their glory teams were gone, except for Gonzo. Pitcher Shawn Estes, once a promising Giants southpaw, was brought in. Kerry Ligtenberg, who had once been thought of as the Braves' closer but had never quite succeeded, was in Arizona. Another former Brave who had seen better days, Javier Lopez, was on the roster.

Pitcher Russ Ortiz had been a winner in San Francisco and Atlanta. Brandon Webb looked promising. Tim Worrell was rumored to have pitched to Ted Williams once. Royce Clayton was a D'back. He had fallen faster than Milli Vanilli after their lip sync episode. Craig Counsell was still around to tell Irish stories. Troy Glaus was typical of the new game.

A Southern California native and UCLA All-American, he had everything a player could ask for when he exploded on the scene in Anaheim. He hit monster homers and achieved icon status, powering the Angels past Bonds' Giants in the 2002 World Series. A player like that should have been to his team what Ernie Banks was to the Cubs, Al Kaline to the Tigers. Instead, he somehow was allowed to get away.

A tall, enormous human being who looked capable of hitting the cover off a baseball Roy Hobbs–style, he was now playing in a game

TRIVIA

How many national championships have been won by Arizona college baseball teams?

Answers to the trivia questions are on pages 159–160.

in which the sordid details of steroid abuse hung like a dark cloud over every slugger. In 2005 Congressional hearings shed more ugly light on the subject. It was as if Glaus just wanted to kind of fade away, not making his presence too well known anymore. What a shame.

In 2005 he was in Arizona. A player who looked like the next Mike Schmidt, he was at a crossroads, as was his team.

Infielder Conor Jackson was a prep All-American from L.A.'s San Fernando Valley who had starred at Cal. His dad was the commander of the legal corps on the TV show *JAG*.

Shawn Green arrived in Phoenix. On the field, the D'backs were better than in 2004, but the 2001 champions looked to be ancient history. They finished 77–85 (.475), which in the National League Worst was now good for second place. San Diego won it. They may have been the most unimpressive division champions ever.

All things considered, with expectations lowered, ownership was happy to draw 2,059,424 fans to Chase Field.

Money in baseball had long been out of control. It reminded one of what former Speaker of the House Sam Rayburn had said: "A billion here, a billion there; pretty soon you're talkin' real money." Some guy named Javier Vazquez was paid by the D'backs *$11 million* in 2005 to do...whatever it is guys like Javier Vazquez do. $100 million, $55 million, $11 million—the numbers just sat there in the transactions sections of the sports page—monopoly money, not real. After a certain amount, it's all the same. Once a player is overpaid by $9 or $10 million, it doesn't seem to matter if he is overpaid by $70 million. Who cares anymore?

The players had their riches and now they had to contend with its immoralities. As the disciple Matthew pointed out, "What does it profit a man to have the whole world, if he loses his soul?"

The nouveau riche of sports would have to find a way to live good and decent lives despite the temptations brought on by so much money. Some would. Many would not.

In 2006 Bob Melvin managed the Diamondbacks. The club consisted of shortstop Craig Counsell at leadoff. Second sacker Orlando Hudson had yet to reach his offensive potential. Third baseman Chad Tracy had a solid inside-out swing, but also could turn on a pitch. Gonzo still patrolled left field. Right fielder Shawn Green featured a fluid, picture-book swing and good approach at the plate. First baseman Conor Jackson had a quick bat with an inside-out, short stroke. Catcher Johnny Estrada had been slowed by injuries and had limited pop. Center fielder Eric Byrnes was a line-drive hitter with some pull power who played the game with his hair on fire.

New pitching ace Brandon Webb featured a live sinker with late-breaking movement. Veteran Orlando "El Duque" Hernandez created deception with a unique delivery. Miguel Batista was now, along with Gonzo, the face of Diamondbacks baseball history. Luis Vizcaino had once been an effective pitcher.

DID YOU KNOW . . . That Craig Counsell and Carl Yastrzemski both came out of the University of Notre Dame?

Glaus

Troy Glaus came up a 6'5", 245-pound third baseman possessing the most extraordinary talents. He emerged from north San Diego County, choosing to pursue his education at UCLA instead of going directly into professional ball. He may very well be the greatest baseball player in Bruins history, which is saying something. Jackie Robinson and Chris Chambliss played in Westwood.

In 2002 Glaus got off to a slow start but finished with 30 home runs and 111 runs batted in. So great was his talent and expectations for him, however, that those numbers were considered disappointing, at least until the World Series.

In 2000 and 2001, Glaus combined for 88 home runs.

"Troy's ceiling is amazing," said Angels manager Mike Scioscia. "I think he has more upside than anybody else in this clubhouse."

After winning the MVP award for the 2002 World Series, Glaus announced, "It's a great honor. But this is for the team, not for me. All 25 guys on this roster contributed to our winning."

In 16 '02 postseason games, Glaus hit seven homers. He was impossible to pitch to. No scouting report could determine his weaknesses because, when he got hot, he had none. Up and in? He tomahawked it. Away? He used his power to hit opposite-field dingers. A mistake pitch? Forget about it.

Glaus was a streaky hitter who in mid-season was having trouble making contact. He struck out 29 times in 89 at-bats at one point, mainly because he insisted on trying to pull the ball. He was not using his size and massive strength. But Glaus never let his slump prevent him from giving it all he had.

Troy Glaus is greeted in the dugout after a solo home run in June 2005.

"He's got a great work ethic," said Angels hitting instructor Mickey Hatcher. "In fact, sometimes I have to get him to back off a bit. The thing is, he gets down on himself. He's been put in that category of a superstar, and it really hurts him when he feels he's not helping the team."

Glaus, despite his "campus hunk" looks, was a very shy fellow who was not comfortable giving interviews.

Against New York he slammed three home runs in the '02 division series. His homer in Game 3 of the ALCS with Minnesota was a humdinger. He deposited an outside fastball from J. C. Romero over the right-field fence, the winning run in a tense 2–1 win.

"It was a great piece of hitting, going the other way," stated Twins' catcher A. J. Pierzynski.

After capturing the series MVP, Glaus told the media, "This is why we put all the time and effort in. All the swings against a garage door when you were a kid."

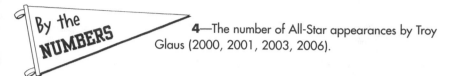

4—The number of All-Star appearances by Troy Glaus (2000, 2001, 2003, 2006).

In a fall classic that at first focused all the attention on the incredible Barry Bonds, it was Glaus with his .385 average (10-for-26), three doubles, three homers, and eight runs batted in that stood tallest in the end.

"At this point, I don't even really know how I'm feeling except ecstatic," he said after the 4–1 seventh game triumph.

"I was just so excited about being world champion. I didn't even really know what to think. These fans have been waiting a long time for this. And I know we're all happy to be part of the team to bring it to them....Actually, we've had that way of thinking all year. No matter what we came up against, we were going to play hard and leave it all out there, and that's what we did here."

Glaus homered in a Game 1, 4–3 loss to San Francisco, as well. It was his two-run double off fireballer Robb Nen in the eighth inning of the unreal sixth game that propelled the team all the way back from a 5–0 deficit to a 6–5 win, which ultimately sucked all the life out of the Giants.

"I think the feeling would be tremendous no matter where we were," he said, "but for me to be home, my friends and family to be here. They've all been a part of it. For them to be watching and the fan support and everything—unbelievable."

In 2004 he slumped to 18 home runs. After hitting only .251 in 2004, Glaus left for Arizona, who picked up his $9 million salary. He played one season in Phoenix, batting .258 with 37 homers and 97 runs batted in during 2005. By the end of the 2006 season, in which he was now with Toronto, Glaus had 257 career home runs in nine seasons.

TRIVIA

Troy Glaus played college ball at UCLA. How many major leaguers have played for the Bruins?

Answers to the trivia questions are on pages 159–160.

Glaus is a player with a pedigree that could land him in Cooperstown, but his record has dropped in recent years. He played one year for the Diamondbacks. He could have been happy in Phoenix, but the game is now about business, not happiness.

Some Promise in Baseball Valley

Six-foot-four, 190-pound outfielder Shawn Green put up great numbers at Toronto in the 1990s. In 2000 he signed with his hometown Los Angeles Dodgers. Green was born in 1972 in Illinois but played at Tustin High School in Orange County, the same school that produced Mark Grace.

He was drafted by the Blue Jays in 1991, a top prep star who was the 16th pick overall. Green made his big-league debut in 1993. In 1995, his first full year, he hit 15 homers. In 1998 he broke through with 35 home runs and 100 runs batted in to go with a .278 average. In 1999 he improved on that, slamming 42 homers with 123 RBIs and a .309 average.

This made him a major free-agent prize. The Dodgers went after him hard. He matched his Toronto output in some years. In 2000 the Dodgers hoped to make their bid, recapturing the dominant position in the National League West. With Arizona slipping from their extraordinary 100-win season of the year before, it was theirs for the taking, but it was San Francisco who asserted their presence.

Green hit 24 homers with 99 RBIs, decent numbers in the Kirk Gibson era but not enough to generate mega-excitement in L.A. In 2001 Green joined the home-run parade of that season with 49, along with 125 runs batted in and a .297 average. The following year he hit 42 longballs with 114 RBIs and a .285 mark. His L.A. production dropped in 2003 and 2004, although in 2004 the Dodgers captured the West from San Francisco on the last day. Green hit 19 and 28 home runs, respectively.

He became a Diamondback in 2005, hitting 22 homers with 73 runs batted in and a .286 batting average in a so-so season. Green

Manager Bob Melvin (left) looks out of the dugout during a 2006 game against the Tampa Bay Devil Rays.

was an All-Star in 1999 and 2002. He won a Gold Glove in the American League in 1999.

Green seemed to have lost some pop by 2005, but he was still considered reliable. He missed just 16 games in six NL seasons and played errorless ball in 2005, despite moving to center for the final two months. He was moved back to right field, where he was more comfortable. In August of 2006, Green was traded to the New York Mets.

Craig Counsell was one of the players from Arizona's glory days. The Diamondbacks dealt Troy Glaus (37 homers) and put Tony Clark (30 homers) on the bench. Counsell was able to do the little things that the new management desired (he stole 26 bases, walked 78 times) and was versatile. He moved from second to short.

The bullpen was a problem, posting a 4.84 ERA (a mark that left them number 14 of 16 teams in the league) in 2005. It was questionable that it could improve with Jason Grimsley and Luis Vizcaino. The rotation lacked depth. The Diamondbacks traded Javier Vazquez, but Brandon Webb proved much better. Orlando

Hernandez was old and injury-prone. Miguel Batista was back to the place he once belonged. Arizona overpaid for Russ Ortiz.

The Diamondbacks were a second-place team despite a 77–85 record, which marked a 26-game improvement over 2004. Luis Gonzalez was one of five big leaguers with a .300 average, 200 doubles, 200 homers, 700 RBIs, and 500 walks since 1999. The others: Brian Giles, Todd Helton, Manny Ramirez, and Alex Rodriguez.

The Diamondbacks thought so highly of Conor Jackson that they planned to play him ahead of Tony Clark, who homered every 11.63 at-bats. Jackson, a significant part of the team's youth movement, hit .354 with 73 RBIs in 93 games for Triple-A Tucson.

New ace Brandon Webb is a 6'2", 228-pound, right-handed pitcher who played at the University of Kentucky, the same school that produced Oakland pitcher Joe Blanton. He came up in 2003.

Born in Ashland, Kentucky, in 1979, Webb was an eighth-round pick by Arizona in 2000. He was 10–9 with a 2.84 ERA with one shutout in 2003. In 2004 Brandon was 7–16, but in 2005 he rebounded for a 14–12 record with a 3.54 ERA. His 2006 stats remained solid (16–8, 3.10 ERA, and the Cy Young Award). The Diamondbacks could have used Webb in 1999 and 2002, when Johnson, and later Johnson-Schilling were just not enough to get them over the playoff hump.

Manager Bob Melvin is, like Bob Brenly, a former San Francisco Giants catcher. He played for Bob Milano at the University of California. The 6'4", 205-pounder came up to the big leagues in 1985. Born in 1961 in the San Francisco Bay Area, he was drafted by Detroit. He played 10 years, including three in San Francisco (1986–1988). After three seasons of splitting time with Mickey Tettleton (1989–1990) and Chris Hoiles (1991) behind the plate for the Baltimore Orioles, Melvin was traded to Kansas City for Storm Davis. He batted a career-high .314 in 1992 but played in only 32 games, never again seeing regular action in his three remaining seasons. He retired after the 1994 season with a .233 career average.

IF ONLY . . . Troy Glaus could have been retained, combined with Shawn Green and Brandon Webb the D'backs might have approached the glory days of 1999–2002.

Melvin stayed in the game, making his big-league managerial debut trying to pick up the pieces of Lou Piniella's Seattle Mariners. One of the best teams ever assembled, the 2001 Mariners failed to capture the brass ring and by 2003 were a remnant of their old selves. Piniella was gone, and Melvin steered the club to a 93–69 mark, good for second place in the competitive American League West. They were behind Oakland but ahead of defending world champion Anaheim. But after that it was downhill. The 93–69 record was reversed (63–99) in 2004.

In 2005 Melvin came to Phoenix. He was 77–85, curiously a contending record in a down West year. He had the D'backs in contention with San Diego in 2006 until they tailed off down the stretch.

Good executive leadership, enthusiastic fan support, and great players have marked the history of the Diamondbacks. In recent years they have experienced failure, a crossroads and now some promise in baseball valley.

ALL-TIME TEAM

Diamondbacks

Position	Name
Pitcher	Curt Schilling
Pitcher	Randy Johnson
Pitcher	Miguel Batista
Pitcher	Brandon Webb
Catcher	Damian Miller
First Base	Mark Grace
Second Base	Jay Bell
Third Base	Matt Williams
Short Stop	Tony Womack
Outfield	Luis Gonzalez
Outfield	Steve Finley
Outfield	Shawn Green
Manager	Bob Brenly

Answers to Trivia Questions

Page 4: Bobby Winkles told Reggie Jackson, when asked if Winkles had put him on the team, "I think we can find a place for you here."

Page 8: State Senate Bill 1344 created the opportunity to bring the MLB to Phoenix. Brought forth by Arizona Republican Representative Chris Herstam, it was an amendment to a bill issuing a bond to overhaul Scottsdale Stadium. His rider created a stadium-funding mechanism. He pushed it through the legislature at the 11th hour in 1989, just before his retirement.

Page 15: Jerry Colangelo was named "Arizona's Most Influential Sports Figure of the 20th Century."

Page 17: Travis Lee was voted the Diamondbacks' Rookie of the Year in 1998.

Page 25: Coyotes, Barracudas, Scorpions, and Rattlers were all considered for the team name. Colangelo preferred Diamondbacks.

Page 28: The Diamondbacks hold spring training in Tucson Electric Park.

Page 33: Thom Brennaman, one of the best in the business, is the play-by-play broadcaster for the Diamondbacks. In addition to his D'backs radio duties, he has worked with FOX Sports and has a national following in baseball and football. Brennaman's father is the legendary Marty Brennaman, longtime voice of the Cincinnati Reds.

Page 40: Omar Daal (2.88) was Arizona's ERA leader in 1998.

Page 45: Luis Gonzalez had 206 hits in 1999.

Page 55: Matt Williams appeared on the show *Arli$$*.

Page 60: Luis Gonzalez played for the University of South Alabama, where he was a Baseball America All-Freshman Second-Team All-American, and later elected to that school's Hall of Fame.

Page 70: Mike Morgan made his big-league debut in June of 1978, one week after graduating from Valley High School in Las Vegas, where he was 7-1 with a 0.68 ERA and 111 K's in 72 innings. He was the number one selection in the draft by Oakland owner Charley O. Finley. Morgan lost to Mike Flanagan and Baltimore 3-0 at the Oakland-Alameda County Coliseum.

Page 77: Greg Swindell set the NCAA record for most shutouts, with 14 between 1984 and 1986.

Page 90: The Yankees had 26 world championships entering the 2001 World Series. No athletic organization—pro, college, or high school—has won as many championships. No team has won that many NBA titles, Super Bowls, NFL titles, or Stanley Cups. No country has been the medal leader in that many Olympics. No collegiate football program has won that many national championships. No high school has won that many national championships in any sport. The only comparison is the USC track and field program with 26 NCAA titles, hardly the same thing. Total pro championships in Arizona entering 2001: Diamondbacks, Suns, Cardinals: 0. Arizona State football: 0. Only the University of Arizona with the 1997 NCAA basketball crown had brought ultimate glory to the state (although ASU and U of A did have a number of College World Series championships between them).

Page 96: The singing of "God Bless America" during the seventh-inning stretch was started after 9/11 and still continues today.

Page 97: The combined record of Randy Johnson and Curt Schilling in the 2001 Fall Classic was 4–0 (Johnson 3–0, Schilling 1–0) with a 1.40 ERA and 45 strikeouts in 38⅔ innings.

Page 114: Yes, Randy Johnson has thrown a perfect game. On May 18, 2004, the Big Unit tossed a perfecto at Atlanta 2–0. He was 40 years old when he did it.

Page 116: Mark Grace was teamed up with actor Bill Murray, one of the world's all-time biggest Cubs fans.

Page 125: The Diamondbacks played against St. Louis in the first round of the National League playoffs. The Cards swept them in three games. Their great season was over just like that!

Page 130: Curt Schilling named his two sons Gehrig, named after Yankees great Lou Gehrig, and Grant, named after Civil War hero U. S. Grant.

Page 133: In the 1930s Dominican dictator Rafael Trujillo imported Negro League stars to play there in order to distract the masses from his brutality. Trujillo's army teams, featuring the Alou Brothers and Juan Marichal, were first-rate. When the Marines entered the country in 1965 in response to an uprising against Trujillo, it established an American presence and a baseball pipeline.

Page 141: American missionaries brought baseball to Asia. Big-league star Lefty O'Doul made exhibition trips to Japan in the 1930s. After World War II, General Douglas MacArthur said O'Doul's postwar return and subsequent goodwill baseball tour did more to unite the U.S. and Japan than any policy. U.S. servicemen serving in Asia spread the game to allied countries Taiwan and South Korea.

Page 146: The Arizona State Sun Devils have won eight MVP awards, by Reggie Jackson (1973) and Barry Bonds (seven: 1990, 1992, 1993, 2001, 2002, 2003, 2004). The Pacific 10 Conference, previously known as the PCC and the Pac 8, has produced 12 MVPs. In addition to Jackson and Bonds, these include Jackie Jensen (1958) and Jeff Kent (2000) of California; Fred Lynn (1975) of Southern California; and Jackie Robinson (1949) of UCLA. The SEC has only two. The Big 10 has two.

Page 150: Arizona college baseball teams have won eight national championships. Arizona State has five (1965, 1967, 1969, 1977, 1981). Arizona has three (1976, 1980, 1986). The Pacific 10 has 25 overall including USC with 12, Cal and Stanford with two, Oregon State with one. The SEC: six. The Southwest Conference: four. The Big 12: three.

Page 154: As of 1998, according to www.baseball-reference.com, 62 Bruins have played in the majors.

Arizona Diamondbacks All-Time Roster

Players who have appeared in at least one game with the Diamondbacks.

* Player still active in major league baseball

A

Joel Adamson (P)	1998
Armando Almanza* (P)	2005
Roberto Alomar (2B)	2004
Brian Anderson* (P)	1998–2002
Greg Aquino* (P)	2004–06

B

Carlos Baerga* (2B)	2003–04
Jeff Bajenaru* (P)	2006
Jarred Ball* (OF)	2006
Willie Banks* (P)	1998
Rod Barajas* (C)	1999–2003
Brian Barden* (3B)	2006
Adam Bass* (P)	2006
Rich Batchelor (P)	1998–1999
Miguel Batista* (P)	2000–03, 2005–06
Tony Batista* (3B)	1998–99
Danny Bautista (OF)	2000–04
Jay Bell (SS)	1998–2002
Andy Benes (P)	1998–99
Yamil Benitez (OF)	1998–99
Nick Bierbrodt* (P)	2001
Willie Blair (P)	1997–98
Ricky Bottalico (P)	2003
Brent Brede (OF)	1998
Juan Brito* (C)	2004, 2006
Troy Brohawn (P)	2001

Scott Brow (P)	1998
Neb Brown* (DH)	2006
Brian Bruney* (P)	2004–06
Jason Bulger* (P)	2005
Eric Byrnes* (OF)	2005–06

C

Alex Cabrera* (1B)	2000–01
Alberto Callaspo* (2B)	2006
Chris Capuano* (P)	2003
Dan Carlson (P)	1998–99
Chris Carter* (1B)	2006
Jonathan Castellanos* (P)	2006
Matt Chico* (P)	2006
Randy Choate* (P)	2004–06
Bobby Chouinard* (P)	1998–2000
Ryan Christenson* (OF)	2001
Alex Cintron* (SS)	2001–06
Tony Clark* (1B)	2005–06
Royce Clayton* (SS)	2005
Greg Colbrunn* (1B)	1999–2002, 2004
Jason Conti* (OF)	2000–01
Bryan Corey* (P)	1998
Lance Cormier* (P)	2004–05
Jim Corsi (P)	2000
Jesus Cota* (1B)	2004, 2006
Craig Counsell* (2B)	2000–03, 2005–06
Jose Cruz* (OF)	2005
Juan Cruz* (P)	2006
Midre Cummings* (OF)	2001
Jack Cust* (OF)	2001

D

James D'Antona* (3B)	2006
Jeff DaVanon* (OF)	2006
Omar Daal* (P)	1998–2000
Casey Daigle* (P)	2004, 2006
Doug DeVore* (OF)	2004
David Dellucci* (OF)	1998–2003
Elmer Dessens* (P)	2003–04
Mike DiFelice* (C)	2001
Edwin Diaz* (2B)	1998–99
Mike Dirosa* (C)	2006
Chris Donnels* (3B)	2002
Jared Doyle* (P)	2006
Stephen Drew* (SS)	2006
Erubiel Durazo* (DH)	1999–2002
Chad Durbin* (P)	2004

E

Damion Easley* (2B)	2005–06
Robert Ellis* (P)	2000–01
Alan Embree* (P)	1998
Matt Erickson* (2B)	2006
Bobby Estalella* (C)	2004
Shawn Estes* (P)	2005
Johnny Estrada* (C)	2005–06

F

Jorge Fabregas* (C)	1997–98
Jeff Fassero* (P)	2004
Mike Fetters (P)	2002, 2004
Nelson Figueroa (P)	2000
Steve Finley* (OF)	1999–2004
Ben Ford* (P)	1998
Casey Fossum* (P)	2004
Andy Fox (SS)	1998–2000
John Frascatore (P)	1999
Alex Frazier* (OF)	2006
Mark Freed* (P)	2006
Hanley Frias (SS)	1998–2000

G

Karim Garcia* (OF)	1998
Lino Garcia* (RF)	2006
Steve Garrabrants* (OF)	2006
Jerry Gil* (SS)	2004, 2006
Bernard Gilkey (OF)	1998–2000
Dustin Glant* (P)	2006
Troy Glaus* (3B)	2005
Alberto Gonzalez* (2B)	2006
Carlos Gonzalez* (OF)	2006
Edgar Gonzalez* (P)	2003–06
Enrique Gonzalez* (P)	2006
Luis Gonzalez* (OF)	1999–2006
Clint Goocher* (P)	2006
Andrew Good* (P)	2003–04
Michael Gosling* (P)	2004–05
Mark Grace (1B)	2001–03
Andy Green* (2B)	2004–06
Shawn Green* (OF)	2005–06
Jason Grimsley* (P)	2006
Buddy Groom (P)	2005
Jose Guillen* (OF)	2002
Geraldo Guzman* (P)	2000–01

H

Scott Hairston* (2B)	2004–06
Adam Haley* (2B)	2006
Brad Halsey* (P)	2005–06
Robby Hammock* (C)	2003–05, 2006
Lenny Harris (3B)	1999–2000
Rick Helling* (P)	2002
Felix Heredia* (P)	2006
Matt Herges* (P)	2005
Orlando Hernandez* (P)	2005–06
Koyie Hill* (C)	2004–06
Shea Hillenbrand* (3B)	2003–04
Darren Holmes* (P)	1999–2000
Mark Holzemer* (P)	2002
Adam Howard* (P)	2006
Ken Huckaby* (C)	2001
Orlando Hudson* (2B)	2005–06

J

Conor Jackson* (1B)	2005–06
Steven Jackson* (P)	2006
Kevin Jarvis* (P)	2006
Randy Johnson* (P)	1999–2004
Chris Jones (OF)	1998
Felix Jose* (OF)	2002–03
Jorge Julio* (P)	2006

K

Matt Kata* (2B)	2003–05
Byung-Hyun Kim* (P)	1999–2003
Chris Kinsey* (P)	2006
Danny Klassen* (3B)	1998–2002
Eric Knott* (P)	2001
Mike Koplove* (P)	2001–06
Josh Kroeger* (OF)	2004
Jeff Kubenka* (P)	1999–2000

L

Sean Lawrence* (P)	2001–02
Travis Lee* (1B)	1998–2000
Kerry Ligtenberg* (P)	2005
Mark Little* (OF)	2002
Albie Lopez* (P)	2001
Javier Lopez* (P)	2005
Brandon Lyon* (P)	2005–06

M

Matt Mantei* (P)	1999–2004
Barry Manuel (P)	1998
Damon Mashore (OF)	2000
Brent Mayne (C)	2004
Quinton McCracken* (OF)	2002–03, 2004–05
Brandon Medders* (P)	2005–06
Hensley Meulens (OF)	1998
Chris Michalak* (P)	1998
Matt Mieske (OF)	2000
Damian Miller* (C)	1998–2002
Jereme Milons* (CF)	2006
Garrett Mock* (P)	2006

Chad Moeller* (C)	2001–03
Mike Mohler (P)	2001
Raul Mondesi (OF)	2003
Miguel Montero* (C)	2005–06
Matt Morgan* (1B)	2006
Mike Morgan (P)	2000–02
Terry Mulholland* (P)	2006
Agustin Murillo* (3B)	2006
Bill Murphy* (P)	2005–06
Neal Musser* (P)	2006
Mike Myers* (P)	2002–03

N

Shane Nance (P)	2004
Cesar Nicolas* (1B)	2006
Dustin Nippert* (P)	2005–06
Vladimir Nunez* (P)	1998–99, 2005

O

Gregg Olson (P)	1998–99
Tim Olson* (3B)	2004
Eddie Oropesa* (P)	2002–03
Russ Ortiz* (P)	2005–06
Lyle Overbay* (1B)	2001–03
Micah Owings* (P)	2006

P

Vicente Padilla* (P)	1999–2000
Jim Parque* (P)	2004
Jose Parra* (P)	2002
Bronswell Patrick* (P)	2002
John Patterson* (P)	2002–03
Tony Pena* (P)	2006
Kenny Perez* (3B)	2006
Ricky Pickett (P)	1998
Dan Plesac (P)	1999–2000
Dante Powell (OF)	1998–99
Bret Prinz* (P)	2001–03

Q

Carlos Quentin* (OF)	2006

R

Brady Raggio* (P)	2003
Stephen Randolph* (P)	2003–04
Dennys Reyes* (P)	2003
Shane Reynolds (P)	2004
Armando Reynoso (P)	1998–2003
Danny Richar* (2B)	2006
Mike Robertson (1B)	1998
Felix Rodriguez* (P)	1997–98
Matt Ruebel (P)	1998–99
Johnny Ruffin* (P)	2000
Rob Ryan* (OF)	1999–2001

S

Erik Sabel* (P)	1999, 2001
Donnie Sadler* (OF)	2004, 2006
Duaner Sanchez* (P)	2002
Reggie Sanders* (OF)	2001
Curt Schilling* (P)	2000–03
Mike Schultz* (P)	2005–06
Scott Service (P)	2003, 2004
Richie Sexson* (1B)	2004
Doug Slaten* (P)	2005–06
Aaron Small* (P)	1998
Chris Snyder* (C)	2004–06
Clint Sodowsky* (P)	1997–99
Juan Sosa* (OF)	2001
Steve Sparks* (P)	2004
Junior Spivey* (2B)	2001–03
Russ Springer* (P)	1998, 2000–01
Andy Stankiewicz (2B)	1998
Kelly Stinnett* (C)	1998–2000, 2005
Todd Stottlemyre (P)	1998–2002
Jeff Suppan* (P)	1997–98
Dale Sveum (SS)	1999
Greg Swindell (P)	1998–2002

T

Amaury Telemaco* (P)	1998–99
Luis Terrero* (OF)	2003–2006
Chad Tracy* (3B)	2004–06

U

Justin Upton* (SS)	2006

V

Efrain Valdez (P)	1998
Jose Valverde* (P)	2003–06
Claudio Vargas* (P)	2005–06
Javier Vazquez* (P)	2005
Brandon Villafuerte* (P)	2004
Oscar Villarreal* (P)	2003–05
Luis Vizcaino* (P)	2005–06
Ed Vosberg* (P)	1999

W

Turner Ward* (OF)	1999–2000
Brandon Webb* (P)	2003–06
Neil Weber (P)	1998–99
Bill White* (P)	2006
Devon White (OF)	1998
Matthew Wilkinson* (P)	2006
Marland Williams* (OF)	2006
Matt Williams (3B)	1997–2003
Desi Wilson (1B)	1998–99
Bobby Witt (P)	2001
Bob Wolcott (P)	1998
Tony Womack* (2B)	1999–2003
Tim Worrell* (P)	2005

Y

Ernie Young* (OF)	1999

Z

Jon Zeringue* (OF)	2006
Alan Zinter* (1B)	2004

Notes

Birth Pangs in the Desert

In an act that endeared Colangelo to millions of Arizonans, the D'backs owner said to Bonds, "I won't be ready for you," then got on an elevator, leaving the speechless Bonds in his wake. (Sherman, Len, *Big League, Big Time.* New York: Pocket Books, 1998.)

Man in the Middle

"I grew up on the south side of Chicago in the 1940s and '50s in an area called Chicago Heights," he said. (Sherman.)

Laying the Groundwork

"I respect the game so much," Showalter said. (Sherman.)

Baseball Valley

"I've got two more years left here, and then I'm coming down, playing with the Diamondbacks," he boldly stated during spring training in 1996. (Sherman.)

Joe Junior

"My first involvement in baseball here came in the mid-'80s," Garagiola Jr. recalled. (Page, Bob, *Tales from the Diamondback Dugout.* Champaign, Il.: Sports Publishing, 2002.)

The Bell Curve

"I grew up all over the world," said Bell. (Page.)

Gonzo

One day during batting practice teammate Bobby Higginson told him, "You gotta learn to hook the ball to play in this park to take advantage of the short porch in right." (www.baseballlibray.com)

Steve Finley

"The one thing about this team," he said of the clubhouse humor in Phoenix, "is that there's nobody immune to the abuse and punishment." (Page.)

Big Unit was a Bay Area Boy of Summer

"Dedeaux was larger than life," recalled Johnson. (Travers, Steven, "Big Unit: Memories of A Simpler Time," *StreetZebra,* June 1999.)

"I never thought about that," said Johnson. (Travers, Steven.) "Big Unit was Bay Area Boy of Summer," *San Francisco Examiner,* April 1, 2001.

"He was the sharpest tack in the box," said his successor, Mike Gillespie. (Travers, Steven, "Talking Heads: Mike Gillespie," *StreetZebra,* June 1999.)

The Price of Victory

"The attitude on this club was 'Geez, you know, we can't believe this happened again!'" Williams recalled. (Page.)

Victory

"Relieving in the seventh game of the World Series wasn't that big a deal to me," Johnson modestly said. (Page.)

Amazing Gracie

Winning the Series was "definitely the highest point of my life, especially for a lot of guys this late in their careers," he said. (Page.)

Christian Soldier

"I knew with that type of delivery," said Sanders, "I could go on his first move." (www.baseballlibrary.com)

"I think we were playing St. Louis." (Page.)

The Hero

"As much as I would have liked to have him pitch," said Francona, "I told him I thought he might regret that later." (www.baseballlibrary.com)

The Philosopher

"I never even played baseball until I was 15 years old," he said. (Page.)

Byung-Hyun Kim

"Dennis Eckersley was scared to death of failure," A's announcer Bill King said in 2001. (Travers, Steven, "A King Walks Amongst Us," *San Francisco Examiner*, May 18, 2001.)

"Rollie was too dumb to know any better," said former teammate Rick Monday. (Travers, Steven, *Dodgers Essential*, Chicago: Triumph Books, 2007.)

Crossroads

"We're committed to going into next season with as close to a bulletproof bullpen as we can get." (Gilbert, Steve, www.mlb.com, October 2, 2005.)

Glaus

"Troy's ceiling is amazing," said Angels manager Mike Scioscia. "I think he has more upside than anybody else in this clubhouse." (Travers, Steven, *Angels Essential*, Chicago: Triumph Books, 2007.)

Library of Congress Cataloging-in-Publication Data

Travers, Steven.
Diamondbacks essential : everything you need to know to be a real fan!
/ Steven Travers.
    p. cm.
Includes bibliographical references.
ISBN: 978-1-57243-944-3
1. Arizona Diamondbacks (Baseball team)—History. I. Title.
GV875.A64T73 2007
796.357'640979173--dc22
                        2006033400

This book is available in quantity at special discounts for your group or organization. For further information, contact:

Triumph Books
542 South Dearborn Street
Suite 750
Chicago, Illinois 60605
(312) 939-3330
Fax (312) 663-3557

Printed in U.S.A.
ISBN: 978-1-57243-944-3
Editorial Production by Prologue Publishing Services, LLC
Design by Patricia Frey
All photos courtesy of AP/Wide World Photos except where otherwise indicated.

DIAMONDBACKS
ESSENTIAL

Everything You Need to Know
to Be a Real Fan!

Steven Travers

TRIUMPH
BOOKS